POWAY HIGH SCHOOL LIBRARY

DATE DUE

What Muslims Think and How They Live

Introducing Islam

The American Encounter
with Islam

Heroes and Holy Places

Islam: The Basics

Islam, Christianity, and
Judaism

Islamic Fundamentalism

Muslims and the West

What Muslims Think
and How They Live

Who Are the Muslims?

What Muslims Think
and How They Live

Rick Hodges

Produced by OTTN Publishing, Stockton, New Jersey

Mason Crest Publishers
370 Reed Road
Broomall, PA 19008
www.masoncrest.com

3 5 7 9 8 6 4 2

#31

Library of Congress Cataloging-in-Publication Data

Hodges, Rick.
  What Muslims think and how they live / Rick Hodges.
    p. cm. — (Introducing Islam)
Includes bibliographical references and index.
  ISBN 1-59084-702-4
1. Islam—Juvenile literature. 2. Muslims—Juvenile literature. [1. Islam. 2.
Muslims.] I. Title. II. Series.
  BP161.3 .H64 2004
  297—dc22
                                              2003023821

Contents

Introduction...6

Polling the Islamic World......................9

The Roots of the
Modern Islamic World..........................15

What it Means
To Be a Muslim Today...........................29

Views on Culture and Values.................43

Women and Islam.....................................61

Views on the Issue
of Palestine...71

Views of the United States
on Other Issues.......................................87

Chronology..100

Glossary..103

Further Reading.................................105

Internet Resources..............................106

Index..107

Contributors..112

Introduction

The central belief of Islam, one of the world's major religions, is contained in a simple but powerful phrase: "There is no god but Allah, and Muhammad is His prophet." The Islamic faith, which emerged from the Arabian desert in the seventh century C.E., has become one of the world's most important and influential religions.

Within a century after the death of the Prophet Muhammad, Islam had spread throughout the Arabian Peninsula into Europe, Africa, and Asia. Today Islam is the world's fastest-growing religion and Muslims can be found throughout the globe. There are about 1.25 billion Muslims, which means that approximately one of every five people follows Islam. The global total of believers has surpassed two older religions, Hinduism and Buddhism; only Christianity has more followers.

Muslims can also be found in North America. Many Muslims have immigrated to the United States and Canada, and large numbers of people—particularly African Americans—have converted to Islam since the 1960s. Today, there are an estimated 6 million Muslims in the United States, with an additional half-million Muslims in Canada.

Despite this growing popularity, many people in the West are uninformed about Islam. For many Americans, their only exposure to this important religion, with its glorious history and rich culture, is through news reports about wars in Muslim countries, terrorist attacks, or fundamentalist denunciations of Western corruption.

The purpose of the INTRODUCING ISLAM series is to provide an objective examination of Islam and give an overview of what Muslims believe, how they practice their faith, and what values they hold most important. Four volumes in particular focus on Islamic beliefs and religious practices. *Islam: The Basics* answers the essential questions about the faith and provides information about the major sects. *Islam, Christianity, Judaism* describes and explains the similarities and differences between these three great monotheistic religions. *Heroes and Holy Places* gives information about such important figures as Muhammad and Saladin, as well as shrines like Mecca and Jerusalem. *Islamic Fundamentalism* focuses on the emergence of the Islamist movement during the 20th century, the development of an Islamist government in Iran, and the differences between Islamists and moderates in such countries as Algeria, Indonesia, and Egypt.

Two volumes in the series explore Islam in the United States, and the relationship between the Muslim world and the West. *The American Encounter with Islam* provides specific history about Muslims in North America from the 17th century until the present, and traces the development of uniquely American sects like the Nation of Islam. *Muslims and the West* attempts to put the encounter between two important civilizations in broader perspective from a historical point of view.

Recent statistical data is extensively provided in two volumes, in order to discuss life in the Muslim world. *Who Are the Muslims?* is a geopolitical survey that explores the many different cultures that can be found in the Muslim world, as well as the different types of Islamic governments. *What Muslims Think and How They Live* uses information collected in a landmark survey of the Islamic world by the Gallup Organization, as well as other socioeconomic data, to examine Muslim attitudes toward a variety of questions and issues.

As we enter a new century, cultural and political tensions between Muslims and non-Muslims continue. Now more than ever, it is important for people to learn more about their neighbors of all faiths. It is only through education and tolerance that we will be able to build a new world in which fear and mistrust are replaced with brotherhood and peace.

Thousands of Muslims participate in Friday prayers at the Khadimiya Shrine in Baghdad, Iraq.

Polling the Islamic World

About a billion and a quarter people throughout the world follow the religion called *Islam*, and are therefore known as *Muslims*. Muslims make up about one-fifth of the world's population and live in practically every country in the world. However, most of the world's Muslim population is concentrated in an area that stretches across thousands of miles, from western Africa to the Philippines and China. This region, which includes more than fifty countries, is often referred to as the Islamic world or the Muslim world.

At the center of the Islamic world is the Middle East, which includes the Arabian Peninsula (once called Arabia) where Islam was born about 1,400 years ago.

9

Most Muslims are not Arabs—it is estimated that only about 18 percent of Muslims in the world are Arabs. The majority of Muslims come from non-Arab Asian and African countries. The country with the largest Muslim population is Indonesia, which is thousands of miles to the east of the Arabian Peninsula.

Because Muslims can be found all over the world, there are wide disparities in the ways that Muslims live. Some Muslims are quite wealthy, but many have barely enough to survive. Lifestyle and devotion to religion also varies broadly across the Islamic world. In places like Saudi Arabia and Iran, the people live according to strict religious codes. In Turkey, the lifestyles of many people are similar to that of a typical town in eastern Europe. Muslims speak hundreds of different languages, follow many different customs, wear different styles of clothes, belong to various ethnic groups, and lead many different kinds of lives.

As with most religions and cultures in the world, there are Muslims who see the rules of Islam as strict and others who see them as flexible and accommodating. There are Muslims who follow religious rules carefully, as part of their daily lives, and others who do not closely observe the rules. And there are a few Muslims who believe extreme behavior, including violence, is acceptable, although most others agree it is forbidden.

There is much for westerners to learn about the way Muslims live and the attitudes and opinions of people living in Islamic countries. In 2001–02, the Gallup Organization, a public-opinion polling company, conducted an unprecedented study that provides interesting insights into the attitudes and beliefs of people throughout the Islamic world. To conduct the poll, the Gallup Organization interviewed more than 10,000 people in nine predominantly Islamic countries—Indonesia, Iran, Jordan, Kuwait, Lebanon, Morocco, Pakistan, Saudi Arabia, and Turkey. In undertaking this enormous project, the Gallup Organization was aided by the Pan Arab Research Center, an affiliated organization founded in 1976 that is headquartered in Dubai, United Arab Emirates. The interviewers asked each person about 120 questions about their views on things like politics, culture, and family life. In Iran and Saudi Arabia, both very important Islamic religious centers, this may have been the first time a public-opinion poll was taken on these sensitive questions.

Though the number of people interviewed is a small fraction of the total population of the Islamic world, the people polled in each country were scientifically selected so that the group is representative of the total adult (over age 18) population of that country. Therefore, their answers and opinions can be interpreted to help understand the views of Muslims living throughout the greater Islamic world. "What is provided [by the Gallup data], therefore, is not merely a brief glimpse at the views of 'elites,' of diplomats, of pundits, or of residents of selected urban areas," explained

Muslim Americans march in support of the United States in Brooklyn on September 21, 2001. Even though most Muslims in the U.S. condemned the radical terrorists who carried out the September 11 attacks on the World Trade Center and Pentagon, some innocent Muslim Americans became targets of violence.

Richard W. Burkholder Jr., the Gallup Organization's director of international public research. "Rather, it's an unprecedented window into the perceptions, hopes, and values of adults across the Islamic world."

WHAT MUSLIMS MOST RESENT ABOUT THE WEST

	Iran	Pakistan	Indonesia	Lebanon	Kuwait	Turkey	Jordan	Morocco
Social aspects: too free, low morals, free sex, aggressive, impolite to elders/parents, dislocation of family relations	45%	50%	38%	59%	58%	34%	71%	34%
Negative attitude toward Arabs/Muslims	1%	18%	4%	8%	15%	9%	16%	5%
High crime rate, drugs, violence, alcoholism, corruption	14%	5%	4%	20%	9%	2%	10%	12%
Arrogance, think they are the best/most powerful/advanced/civilized	2%	4%	20%	10%	3%	16%	7%	2%
Underestimate small/poor countries, do not care about them	1%	—	6%	5%	4%	2%	3%	33%
Interference in other countries' internal affairs, politics monopoly/dictatorship	5%	1%	4%	6%	5%	1%	8%	13%
Not attached to their own religion/beliefs/ethinicity	3%	9%	1%	8%	4%	3%	9%	0%
Number of Interviews	1,501	2,043	1,050	1,050	790	1,019	797	1,000

Note: Question not asked in Saudi Arabia.   Source: The Gallup Organization.

The Gallup poll data provides insights into trends and general ideas in the Islamic world, but there are significant variations among the nine countries surveyed. Also, these nine countries cannot be considered to represent all Muslims—a fact that must be taken into consideration when analyzing the data. In this book, the Gallup Poll and other sources are cited to provide general information on how modern Muslims view their personal lives, their beliefs, and their place in the world. This book will give some background information about the history of Islam and the basic tenets of the faith. It will discuss Muslim views on their daily life and customs, the experiences of Muslim women, and opinions about the United States and the West.

Interviews for the Gallup Poll of the Islamic World began just two months after the September 11, 2001, terrorist attacks on the United States. These attacks destroyed the World Trade Center in New York City and damaged the Pentagon near Washington, D.C., and they have resulted in greater U.S. military involvement in the Islamic world. In the fall of 2001 the United States overthrew the Islamic Taliban government in Afghanistan after accusing it of harboring the terrorists that had plotted the September 11 attacks. This attack on Afghanistan, as well as the spring 2003 invasion of Iraq, another country where a majority of the people are Muslims, angered many people throughout the Islamic world. Especially because of continued U.S. involvement in world affairs, the need for understanding and respecting the world's Muslim population and its views on life in the modern world has never been greater.

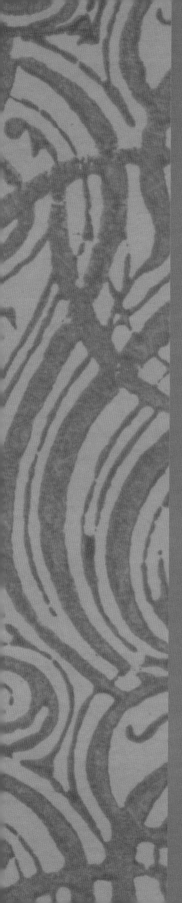

This 17th century Turkish ceramic tile is inscribed with the Muslim creed: "There is no God but Allah, and Muhammad is His Prophet."

The Roots of the Modern Islamic World

Islam was born early in the seventh century, when a man named Muhammad began to receive messages from *Allah*, or God, through an angel. The word Islam is derived from the Arabic verb *aslama*, which means "submitted" or "surrendered." Muslims are expected to surrender to the will of Allah.

Muslims believe Allah is the same God worshiped by Jews and Christians. The Arabs trace their lineage from Abraham, an ancient figure also revered by Jews and Christians, and their heritage includes many stories from the Torah and the Old Testament of the Christian Bible. These holy scriptures are also respected by Muslims, although the Islamic holy book, the *Qur'an*, is revered above them. Muslims consider Muhammad the last in a long line of Abrahamic prophets that includes Isaac, Ishmael, Moses, and Jesus. The messages brought by these prophets were, according to Muslims, misunderstood or distorted by humans, so Allah sent His final, complete message through Muhammad to all humankind.

THE LIFE OF MUHAMMAD

Muhammad was an Arab who lived in the city of Mecca (Makka), which is located in modern-day Saudi Arabia. As a child, Muhammad had been orphaned and had grown up tending sheep and goats. He later became a successful trader, although he never learned how to read or write.

In Muhammad's time, the majority of Arabs worshiped many gods. When he was about 40 years old, around 610 C.E., Muhammad was meditating in a cave when he was visited by the angel Gabriel. The angel told Muhammad that there is only one god, Allah. Muhammad was ordered to proclaim this message to the people of the Arabian Peninsula.

Muhammad soon began to speak to others as Allah directed. He was very critical of the widespread injustice and oppression that prevailed in Mecca, and the message Muhammad preached from Allah was one of equality, justice, compassion, and mercy. The Prophet soon attracted a group of committed followers. Most of Muhammad's early followers were poor people and women. Muhammad's message appealed to them because he wanted to establish a community that would treat all of its members fairly and respectfully.

The wealthy and powerful leaders of Mecca opposed Muhammad's message, fearing that it threatened their livelihoods. They persecuted Muhammad and his followers, passing laws that prohibited all business and social relations between Muslims and non-Muslims. The Meccans took away Muslim homes and properties. As a result, Muslims living in Mecca could not earn a living, and some starved to death.

At the same time, the Meccans targeted and tortured Muslims, especially those who were poor and powerless. Some Muslims were attacked and murdered during this time of unrest. Meccan leaders also plotted to kill Muhammad and his prominent followers, but these plots failed. Ultimately, this oppression forced the Muslims to begin looking for a new home outside of Mecca.

In 620 representatives from Yathrib, an oasis community in Arabia approximately 250 miles north of Mecca, asked Muhammad to come to their city and settle their disputes. Two tribes of the region, Aws and Khazraj, had been engaged in violent warfare for many years, and wanted Muhammad to help them resolve their differences. In 622, after the plot to assassinate Muhammad was uncovered, Muhammad and the Muslims left Mecca and moved to Yathrib. This important event is known as the *hijra*, from an Arabic word meaning to migrate or to leave one's tribe.

In the Arab world of the seventh century, this was a major decision. The tribe was the basis of Arab society. Members of a tribe considered themselves bound by moral and social obligations in addition to family ties. When Muhammad and his followers left Mecca, they abandoned their responsibilities to other members of their tribe. The relatives they left behind in Mecca vowed to destroy the Muslims who had rejected their families and traditions.

When Muhammad arrived in Yathrib, he helped the feuding tribal leaders settle their differences. Then the Prophet and his companions established the first Muslim community (*umma*). The first **mosque** was built next to Muhammad's house, and it became the center of religious and social activity for the Muslims. Even though Muhammad did not force any of the city's inhabitants to convert to Islam, many people chose to become Muslims. Islamic ideas soon became the basis of the city's judicial and social systems. The name of the city was eventually changed to Medina (which means "city," but has been interpreted to mean "city of the Prophet").

In Islamic thought the *umma* is the basis of all social relations. Membership in the *umma* is more binding than membership in a

family or tribe. Members of the *umma* must protect and defend
each other regardless of their previous tribal relations. This pact
of mutual defense applied to the entire community—Muslim and

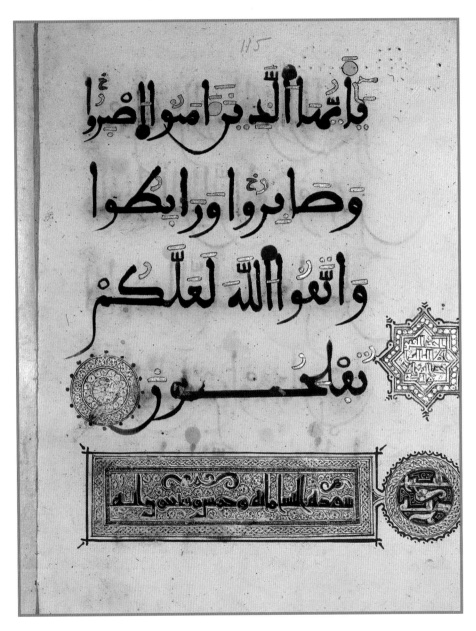

An ornate page from a copy of the Qur'an that dates back to the 13th century. The verse shown in Arabic here reads, "O ye who believe, persevere in
patience and constancy."

non-Muslim. If any group within the *umma* was threatened, the rest of the *umma* was obligated to defend them. The concept of *umma* supplanted the traditional Arab notion of obligations based on blood relationships. Acceptance of this new social ideal was an important act of faith for the Muslims and for the non-Muslims who lived among them in Medina.

The Muslims at Medina and their allies were at war with the Meccans from 624 to 628, when a peace treaty was negotiated. In 629 the Meccans broke the treaty and the war resumed. The fighting ended in 630 when Muhammad led an army of 10,000 Muslims and their allies to Mecca. Disheartened, outnumbered, and surrounded, the Meccans surrendered without a fight. After the conquest of Mecca, many people living in the city decided to become Muslims. Muhammad continued to teach the messages revealed from Allah until he died peacefully two years later.

On the Arabian Peninsula at the time of the Prophet, information was preserved primarily through memorization, rather than writing. During Muhammad's lifetime, many of his companions memorized his teachings verbatim. In the years after Muhammad's death, these teachings were written down and organized as the Qur'an—the holy book of Islam. The early Muslims went to great lengths to preserve the exact wording and organization of Allah's teachings, and Muslims believe the text of the Qur'an is the literal, unchanged word of Allah, given through Muhammad, his prophet and messenger. The Qur'an explains what is required to be a Muslim and to live a good life. Although the holy book has been translated into English and other languages, Muslims maintain that the Qur'an can only be truly understood when read in Arabic. Even today, many Muslims memorize the entire Qur'an.

THE RAPID SPREAD OF A NEW RELIGION

After Muhammad's death, his followers gathered huge armies, first conquering all the Arabs and then defeating many surrounding nations. The Muslims won nearly every battle, and in a remarkably short period they established a vast empire that stretched from Spain in the west to China in the east. The Muslims felt that Allah blessed and supported their efforts. This sentiment is supported by the Qur'an, which consistently told Muslims not to fear or worry because Allah was with them and would give them victory if they were true believers.

The Muslims wanted to spread their religion throughout the world, as Allah commanded. As the Arab armies won victories, they offered the vanquished peoples an opportunity to convert to Islam. This conversion was supposed to be a free decision. The Qur'an says that non-Muslims cannot be forcibly converted, and gives Jews and Christians, known as *ahl al-kitab* ("the people of the book") or *ahl al-dhimma* ("the protected people"), more respect than followers of other religions, because these two groups worship the same God that Muslims worship. The people of the book who wanted to continue following their faiths were given certain rights in the Islamic state, and were required to pay a tax in return. However, many people living under Muslim rule eventually adopted Islam.

It is worth noting that the spread of Islam was driven by more than just military conquest. The enlightened Islamic culture was attractive to many people, particularly when compared to the repressive and at times barbaric systems of thought that had prevailed in other parts of the region at the time. In some areas, trade and the exchange of goods and ideas played a more central role in the spread of the religion than did warfare, particularly as Islam spread into Asia.

The Islamic empire contained many great cities, some with impressive libraries, universities, monuments, and public buildings, and harbored people of many different cultures, including Roman, Greek, Persian, Jewish, and Hindu. The Muslims absorbed the knowledge and culture of many of these peoples and combined them with their own traditions to form new civilizations. They made many new advances in architecture, science, medicine, and mathematics. Europeans learned a great deal from

A Shiite bows his head in prayer. A schism in the Muslim community occurred after the death of Ali, the fourth caliph, in 661 and the massacre of his son Hussein at the Battle of Karbala in 680.

Muslim societies. For instance, the symbols we use to represent numbers today (1, 2, 3, etc.) were borrowed from the Arabic mathematical system. Muslim intellectuals also preserved many ancient books about philosophy and science by translating them into Arabic. The most important of these books are those of Plato, Aristotle, and Plotinus.

DIVISION OF MUSLIMS INTO SECTS

An important event in Islamic history is the division of Muslims into two major groups. This schism became a source of conflict that pitted Muslim against Muslim, and differences between the two groups persist today.

After Muhammad's death, his followers disagreed about who would lead the Muslims. One group believed that the succession of leadership should be hereditary, and wanted to choose a leader from Muhammad's family. They supported Muhammad's son-in-law, Ali, to be the Muslim leader. Most Muslims, however, believed that the leader should be a person of great faith chosen from the Muslim community, and selected a man named Abu Bakr to be the first *khalifa* (**caliph**, or "successor"). This indicated that succession would be based on the piety of the leader, rather than on heredity.

Ali was eventually elected caliph in 656, but he was assassinated in 661. Ali's supporters claimed that his son Hussein should become caliph. However, Hussein and a group of his followers were massacred at the Battle of Karbala in 680. This smaller group of Muslims who followed Ali and his family became known as **Shiites**. The name *Shiite* comes from the Arabic word *shia*, meaning party. In time, the word came to be used primarily in connection with Ali. Thus, Shiites came to mean the party or followers of Ali. The larger group of Muslims are known as **Sunni**, from an Arabic word meaning "the path," because they follow the path they believe Muhammad set for them.

Today, about 85 percent of Muslims are Sunnis, while about 14 percent are Shiites. Many Shiites live in Iran, Iraq, Lebanon, and Bahrain; there are smaller populations in Syria, Pakistan, India, and Azerbaijan. Although Sunnis and Shiites disagree about the leadership of the Muslim nation, the members of both groups obey the Qur'an and follow the principles of Islam.

CRUSADES AND COLONIALISM

In the eighth century Muslim armies had moved from Africa across the Mediterranean Sea into Spain, and by the eleventh century they had created an enlightened civilization there. At the same time, Muslim forces were expanding their territories into Eastern Europe as well. In 1095 the leader of the Roman Catholic

Church, Pope Urban II, called on European rulers to send armies east to protect Constantinople, a city in modern-day Turkey that was the center of the Christian Byzantine Empire. Another goal was the capture of Jerusalem from the Muslims, because of the city's religious significance to Christians. The pope's call marked the start of the *Crusades*, a series of invasions by Europeans into territory controlled by Muslims. The invasions continued until the thirteenth century.

Thousands of European knights responded to the call, marching east to Constantinople. Some of them joined the First Crusade for

A Medieval manuscript illustration shows a ship crossing the Mediterranean Sea carrying European knights to fight in the Middle East. The Crusades were a series of wars between Muslims and Christians that occured from 1095 to 1291.

religious reasons, but many participated because they saw an opportunity to seize new lands and increase their personal wealth. By 1099 the Crusaders had fought their way to Jerusalem, capturing it and other cities from the Muslims.

The European knights established small Crusader kingdoms from which they ruled the conquered territory, but Muslims based in Egypt later counterattacked and took back Jerusalem. Over the next two centuries a series of wars in the region pitted Christians against Muslims (and sometimes European Christians against Orthodox Christians living in the Byzantine empire). The Muslims eventually regained control of their Arab territories, but the power of the Arab caliphs was severely weakened.

In the West, the Crusades are often viewed in a positive light, as a glorious struggle to take control over the Holy Land. Muslims view the Crusades in a much different way—as an offensive, unprovoked invasion motivated by a religious fanaticism bent on destroying the Islamic faith. Muslims vividly recall atrocities committed by European knights, such as the massacre of Muslim and Jewish civilians after Jerusalem was captured in 1099, and the murder of 2,700 prisoners by the army of the English king Richard the Lionhearted in 1191.

Even today the Crusades remind Muslims of the danger posed by the West. Although the word "crusade" is often used to refer to a struggle, to Muslim ears the word connotes a religious war against Islam. For example, when President George W. Bush described his government's renewed effort to combat terrorism as a "crusade" shortly after the September 11, 2001, terrorist attacks on the United States, many Muslims were offended. They believed the president was calling for a crusade against their religion, rather than against extremists willing to use terrorism as a political tool.

The spread of European influence after the fifteenth century had an even greater effect on the Islamic world. By the eighteenth and nineteenth centuries, countries like Great Britain, France, Italy, the Netherlands, and Germany had established colonies throughout Africa, Asia, and the Middle East. The Muslims living in the colonies were often discriminated against by their European rulers. The resources of Muslim lands contributed to the growth of the empire, but the European powers did little to help the lives of ordinary people living in their colonies.

When the Ottoman Empire, a large Muslim empire based in Turkey, collapsed at the end of World War I, Britain and France took control of the former Ottoman territories. During the war these two countries had made the secret Sykes-Picot agreement, which divided the Middle East into British and French spheres of influence. The European powers controlled the territories by supporting leaders who followed the policies the French or British imposed. People living in these countries had little input into their government.

During the 1920s and 1930s, independence movements emerged in many of these colonies. The oppressed residents of the colonies protested against their colonial rulers, and these protests at times became violent. Some of these territories became independent in the 1930s; others won their freedom during or after World War II, when the European powers had been weakened by the global struggle. However, the western colonial powers had created their states in Africa and the Middle East by imposing arbitrary borders, which often separated people of similar ethnic backgrounds or religious beliefs. In some places, old enemies were joined together or the colonial rulers had favored one group over another. Once the states gained independence, disputes erupted.

Western involvement in the Islamic world continued even after countries like Indonesia, Algeria, India, Lebanon, and Jordan gained their independence. The United States and European countries sent money, weapons, technology, and occasionally military forces to these countries. Western goals included protecting their access to the Middle East's vast reserves of petroleum and preventing the Soviet Union from gaining influence in the Islamic world. Although the U.S. and some other Western governments claimed that they wanted to promote freedom and democracy in these countries, in reality they often supported oppressive dictators

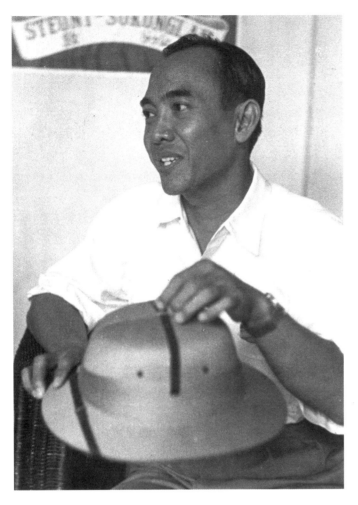

Achmad Sukarno (1902–1970) was the first president of Indonesia after the country became independent in August 1945. During his rule the communist party gradually gained greater power in Indonesia. In the mid-1960s, the U.S. Central Intelligence Agency (CIA) orchestrated a coup that allowed General Suharto, who held pro-American views, to seize power.

who favored the West. In some cases, the U.S. was secretly involved in removing leaders with popular support, such as Iranian Prime Minister Mohammed Mossadegh, who was overthrown in a CIA-supported coup in 1953, and Indonesian President Achmad Sukarno, who was removed from power in the mid-1960s.

The involvement of the West created or worsened a number of conflicts in the Islamic world. This history has caused many Muslims to distrust the West and believe that the United States and other western nations want to dominate Islamic countries.

Since gaining their independence, the people of a few Muslim countries have enjoyed more freedom and a better life. However, many Muslims have suffered as dictators used military power or the threat of harsh punishments to take control. Other governments have been unable or unwilling to stop fighting between groups inside their countries, or to protect one group from hurting another, or to help their people get better education, jobs, or living conditions. Many problems and conflicts remain for Muslims to solve.

A Muslim pauses in a store in New York to pray. The Qur'an and the example of Muhammad's life guide Muslims in proper behavior.

What it Means to be a Muslim Today

The followers of Islam are expected to live every day according to their faith. The Qur'an and other texts based on the sayings and deeds of Muhammad tell Muslims to be honest, respectful, faithful to their spouses, and helpful to the poor or weak.

With a few exceptions, there are no priests or ministers in Islam to instruct the faithful or speak on behalf of Allah. To become a Muslim and fulfill the faith, one simply obeys the commandments of the Qur'an. Throughout the Islamic world, these requirements guide the rhythm of life for millions of people every day.

THE FIVE PILLARS OF ISLAM

The most important requirement in Islam is a belief in one God. There are five important precepts that are observed by all Muslims, known as the five pillars of Islam. The first of these is the simplest: A Muslim announces in Arabic Allah's uniqueness and Muhammad's being a messenger before witnesses who are also Muslims. The announcement is the basic message of Islam, one that every Muslim learns from a very early age: *La ilah illa Allah Muhammad rasul Allah*. This means, "There is no god but Allah, and Muhammad is His messenger."

The second pillar unites Muslims across the world in a ritual that Muslims have had to practice every day since Muhammad's time. At different times during the day—usually at dawn, midday, afternoon, evening, and before bedtime—Muslims are supposed to stop whatever they are doing and pray.

Muslims may pray with others in a mosque (a place of worship) or in their home or office, or even on the sidewalk. The only time Muslim men (and according to some interpretations, Muslim women) are required to pray in a mosque is at mid-day prayers every Friday. Males and females usually pray in separate areas of a mosque.

Cleanliness during prayer is important, and Muslims perform a ritual wash (or ablution) before reciting each of the five required prayers. Muslims who are not at home or in a mosque may place a rug on the ground wherever they are and pray on it. Worshippers remove their shoes before prayer, and on Fridays a large collection of shoes can pile up at the entrance to the prayer area.

To pray, Muslims kneel and then bow their heads to touch the floor several times, always in the direction of Mecca. The prayers and the movements are the same for every Muslim, and when they are praying in a group, Muslims kneel and bow as a group, following the *imam* (prayer leader) who signals each movement by saying *Allahu Akhbar* ("God is greatest").

By tradition, Muslims never make paintings or statues that depict Allah or figures like Muhammad, so that Muslims will not forget that they worship only Allah. Intricate geometric designs and beautiful calligraphic writings adorn the walls of most large mosques. Smaller mosques, especially in the West, cannot afford such decorations and appear simpler.

In Muslim cities and towns across the world, the voice of the *mu'adhdhin* can be heard chanting a call to prayer from the tower of the local mosque at each prayer time. The five required prayers are an important part of a Muslim's day.

Islamic law does not permit Allah to be depicted in drawings, paintings, sculpture, or other artwork. Representations of Muhammad are generally also forbidden; some Muslims believe the human figure itself should never be depicted. Images or icons of Allah, Muhammad, or the saints could lead some people to worship them as idols, a practice strictly forbidden in Islam. Because of the restrictions, over the centuries Muslim artists focused their creativity in other ways, such as the creation of decorative tile patterns and ornate calligraphy.

The third pillar requires Muslims to give to the poor, orphans, widows, or others less fortunate than themselves. Some Islamic countries, such as Pakistan, collect a tax to fulfill this requirement. In other countries, this religious tax is left to the individual Muslims to pay according to their consciences.

The fourth pillar is perhaps the most difficult. For the entire month of *Ramadan*, the ninth month of the Islamic lunar calendar, all Muslims except young children, nursing mothers, travelers, or the sick must abstain from eating, drinking, and other earthly pleasures from sunrise to sunset. The fast during Ramadan honors the month when Muhammad received his first messages

Millions of Muslim pilgrims visit the Great Mosque in Mecca each year. At the far end of the mosque, pictured here during the *hajj* period, the ancient Kaaba can be seen; it looks like a black cube. This is the most sacred shrine in Islam.

from Allah. Ramadan is a time for Muslims to be thankful for what they have, renew their spirit, and make peace with others.

The final pillar is the *hajj,* or pilgrimage to Mecca. Every Muslim is expected to visit the holy city at least once during his or her lifetime, if they are able to make the trip physically and financially. Before air travel made the journey to Mecca easier, Muslims might spend years traveling thousands of miles to reach Mecca. Now more than a million people visit each year. Non-Muslims, however, are forbidden from entering most of Mecca.

Muslims making the pilgrimage wear plain white garments. Everyone is considered to be equal regardless of their wealth or background—even kings and queens wear the same simple clothes as the other pilgrims and live alongside them. While in Mecca, pilgrims do not shave, comb their hair, cut their nails, or wear perfume. By following the same simple lifestyle, the pilgrims stress their unity as Muslims and are reminded that earthly things like wealth and appearance are not very important. They express unity by the sameness of life that they lead in those few days. The simplicity of that life indicates their view of earthly things.

The rituals of the *hajj* last for several days. They include walking seven times around a small building called the Kaaba. The Kaaba is shaped like a cube (the word *kaaba* means "cube" in Arabic) and covered with a black cloth. It has no windows and nothing inside. The Kaaba is located in the center of an outdoor courtyard the size of a football field in the Great Mosque of Mecca. Muslims believe Adam, the first man, built the Kaaba as a place of worship, and that the building was later repaired by Abraham and his son Ishmael. An ancient black stone, called al-Hajar al-Aswad, is located in the eastern wall of the Kaaba. According to one legend, the stone was originally white when it was given to Adam after his fall from Paradise, but it turned black from absorbing the sins of the millions of pilgrims who have touched it over the centuries. Another legend is that the stone was sent from heaven to Abraham—possibly it was a meteorite—and placed in the wall as a marker for pilgrims to determine how many times they had walked around the Kaaba. After the pilgrims have circled the Kaaba seven times, some kiss the stone.

The rituals of the *hajj* are intended to emphasize the unity of Muslims, and to confirm and strengthen the unity of the Abrahamic faiths. This is an important part of the Muslim creed. Muhammad is considered the last in a long line of Abrahamic prophets. The rituals of pilgrimage repeatedly underscore the Muslim belief in the divinity of the messages of all the Abrahamic prophets and the basic unity of those who follow the creed of Abraham.

For nearly every Muslim who makes the trip, the *hajj* is a life-changing event. People from all nations and races, rich and poor, become equals when they travel to Mecca. Making the journey reminds them of the importance of faith in their lives and the need to respect their fellow Muslims. "Elsewhere, except at the best of times, every person looked out for himself," writes Michael Wolfe, an American Muslim who went on a *hajj* in 1990. "During the *Hajj*, people looked out for each other."

The government of Saudi Arabia, where Mecca is located, provides transportation, shelter, food, and guides to help the pilgrims through the rituals. This is an enormous task during the special *hajj* season that occurs for one week each year, when hundreds of thousands of visitors flood the city. Some visitors have died in the crush of the crowds at holy places, from the heat, or owing to other disasters.

OTHER REQUIREMENTS OF ISLAM

A Muslim's duties extend beyond the five pillars. Islam requires believers to show their obedience to Allah in every aspect of life. Some of these social and moral requirements come from the Qur'an. Others are derived from things Muhammad said, actions he took, and even things he did not do. These are known as the Sunna ("custom" or "way") of the Prophet, and include collections of Muhammad's statements, which are called the **Hadith**.

Most Muslim women follow the commandment to cover themselves in public. Veiling can take several forms, from a simple headscarf (*hijab*) to a full-length garment in which only the eyes are visible through mesh (the *burqa*). The *hijab*, worn by the women pictured here, is the most common form of veiling.

Using the Sunna, Muslims can follow Muhammad's example of a near-perfect life and understand the Qur'an better. The Hadith reports were compiled from the memories of Muhammad's followers after he died. (The word *Hadith* can refer to one or more of the reports about Muhammad's Sunna.)

Muslims disagree about the accuracy of some of the Hadith. Sunni and Shiite Muslims have different opinions on how Muslims should behave, and which Hadith are legitimate. Because Sunni Muslims are the largest sect, this section will focus on Sunni beliefs and traditions.

The Qur'an tells believers, "Those who surrender themselves to God and accept the true Faith; who are devout, sincere, patient, humble, charitable, and chaste; who fast and are ever mindful of

God—on these, both men and women, God will bestow forgiveness and a rich reward." (33: 35). This and other passages in the Qur'an, along with similar ones in the Sunna, call on Muslims to live morally upstanding lives. Muslims are expected to give to the poor and to orphaned children, to be courteous to others, to be honest and trustworthy, to refrain from gambling or drinking alcohol, and to defend Islam from attackers. Muslims also value hospitality. Guests to a family's home, whether close friends or strangers, receive food, drink, and high respect.

One of the most visible symbols of Muslim life are the veils that many Muslim women wear in public. These sometimes cover their entire bodies, including their faces. The Qur'an calls on Muslim women to dress modestly. Many Muslim women wear a simple head scarf that covers their hair but not their faces. Other women, particularly those living in countries like Saudi Arabia and Yemen, may wear a full-body robe with only slits for the eyes. Others wear various kinds of veils that cover all or part of their faces. Still other women wear nothing on their faces or hair, or cover their hair only during prayers and in a mosque. Men are also supposed to dress modestly and in many Muslim societies men may wear caps or turbans as signs of their religious devotion.

Islam teaches its followers to enjoy life and its pleasures as gifts from Allah, as long as they remember that the true reward for a good life comes after death.

HOLIDAYS AND CELEBRATIONS

Muslims observe certain celebrations every year with holidays and feasts. They track their holidays by the Islamic calendar, which follows the phases of the moon rather than the circuit of the sun around the earth. Like the Gregorian calendar used in the West, a year in the Islamic calendar includes twelve months; however, because the cycles of the moon and the sun do not quite match, the Islamic year is about eleven days shorter than the 365-day Western year.

The Islamic calendar begins in the year Muhammad left Mecca for Medina (622 C.E. in the Western calendar). Nearly all Muslim countries follow the western calendar for business but use the Islamic calendar to determine the dates of religious holidays.

The most important month of the Islamic calendar is Ramadan. Because the Muslim calendar is based on the movement of the moon instead of the sun, Ramadan occurs in different seasons in different years. When it falls in summer, the wait for nightfall and the breaking of the fast are more difficult because summer days are longer.

When Ramadan is officially over, Muslims greet the end of the fasting with a joyful feast called *Eid al-Fitr* that may last up to three days. They celebrate the holiday by visiting friends and relatives, as well as the graves

Muslims recite prayers over a relative's grave during Eid al-Fitr. This three-day festival marks the end of Ramadan.

of loved ones who have died. They give gifts to their family and to poor people.

Another feast, Eid al-Adha, marks the high point of the month when most Muslims visit Mecca on a pilgrimage. The Muslims visiting Mecca sacrifice an animal on this day as part of their *hajj* ritual. Muslims everywhere else in the world join them by slaughtering a goat, sheep, or other animal to begin the feast. They share the meat with friends, relatives, and the needy.

Muslims in different parts of the world celebrate other annual holidays, such as the birthday of Muhammad and New Year's Day on the Islamic calendar. Shiites mourn the death of Ali's son Hussein, who was murdered in Karbala. They wear mourning clothes, visit the gravesites of important Shiite leaders, and read stories about their fallen ancestors.

The Islamic calendar follows the same seven-day week as the Gregorian calendar. Although Friday is the day of congregational prayer, it is not considered a day of rest to Muslims, like Sunday is to Christians or the Sabbath (Saturday) is to Jews. Still, Muslims in many countries do not work on Fridays, and some countries require businesses and government offices to close on that day of the week.

ISLAMIC LAW

In the early centuries following the death of Muhammad, Muslims established religious rules for living, called **Sharia**. *Sharia* is a legal system based on the Qur'an and three other sources: written narrations about Muhammad's deeds and sayings, the religious scholars' opinions, and analogical reasoning.

Islamic law gives rights and freedom to Muslims as well as rules to follow, and it can change with the times. *Sharia* does not simply say which acts are right and which are wrong—some are only encouraged, discouraged, or simply allowed. In those cases, an individual must decide how to act based on the circumstances.

When Islamic law was created, religion was the only source of the rules governing society. The concept of separating church and state developed much later. Today, most Islamic countries have adopted civil law or common law systems to regulate their societies, and limit *Sharia* to personal and family laws. Countries like Saudi Arabia and Iran purport to base all of their laws on *Sharia*. Countries like Egypt, Syria, Jordan, Iraq, Algeria, Morocco, Tunisia, and Kuwait have adopted the French civil law system, while Pakistan, Sudan, and Indonesia mix Islamic law with the British common law system.

The level of freedom a Muslim enjoys often depends greatly on the rulers of their country. The United States and many western nation-states are democracies in which people have the power to choose their leaders and speak their minds. Only a few Islamic countries give their people a degree of democracy similar to that enjoyed by people in the West. For example, a 2001 study by the pro-democracy group Freedom House showed that only 11 of 47 countries in which the majority of the population is Muslim have democratically elected governments. The study confirmed that 28 Islamic countries give little political or personal freedom to their people.

On the other hand, the study reported that the Muslim countries with democratically elected governments include the countries with the largest Muslim populations—Bangladesh, Indonesia, Turkey, and India. This means that a majority of Muslims live in democratic societies and have at least some opportunity to choose their government leaders.

Saudi Arabia, Iran, and several other countries use strict Islamic beliefs to justify the denial of some rights. Saudi Arabia imposes a strict brand of Islam called Wahhabism. Saudi Arabia is ruled by a monarch and his family (the Al Saud) and has no national legislature that reflects the will of the people. A few Islamic countries, like tiny Brunei in Southeast Asia, are so wealthy that few of their people care about changing or criticizing the government. But other states in the Islamic world suffer under dictators who often ignore both Islamic law and democratic ideals.

One of the most brutal and extreme governments in the Islamic world in recent history was the Taliban regime in Afghanistan. The Taliban imposed its own extremely rigid and harsh version of religious law—stricter even than Saudi Arabia's—after taking power in 1996. Most movies, music, games, and sports were banned; women were forced to cover their entire bodies in public and forbidden from working or going to school; and punishment for even small crimes was severe, including public whippings, amputation of limbs, and executions.

Though human-rights organizations around the world deplored the Taliban's excesses, the government was ultimately brought down after it was accused of sheltering the al-Qaeda terrorists who supposedly had committed the September 11 attacks. The U.S. invaded Afghanistan and eliminated the Taliban govern-ment—a move that was opposed by many people in the Islamic world. U.S. government officials defended the military action as freeing the troubled nation from its oppressive government; critics pointed out the civilian casualties and destruction of Afghan communities.

Some Islamic countries are moving toward greater participation of citizens in government. The small Arab nation of Bahrain, an island in the Persian Gulf, held elections for a new legislature in November 2002. For the first time women were allowed to vote and run for office. Other Arab states, such as Oman and Qatar, have elected councils that advise the rulers. Even reformers in Saudi Arabia are pushing for the creation of a national legislature.

In other Islamic countries, some Muslims feel that their leaders have become corrupt and immoral, or that their systems of govern-ment have taken too much from the legal system and culture of the West. They have called for stricter adherence to Islamic law in gov-ernment. These Muslims have become known as *Islamists* (in the West, they are sometimes also known as Islamic fundamentalists).

Islamists want to make Islam the center of social and political life in their countries. Not all Islamist groups believe this requires less freedom, however. Some believe that Islamic law requires gov-ernments to give Muslims more freedom than they have, and they want to bring democracy or equality to the people of their countries. But other Islamist groups believe that freedom and exposure to Western culture and values has only brought corruption and immorality to their countries and believe that imposing *Sharia* will reverse the trend. Many Islamists have drawn support from Muslims because of their growing distrust of the West.

The Islamist movement has sometimes used peaceful means and elections to try to change their governments. Islamist candidates have won elections in Algeria, Turkey, and other countries. However, the best-known Islamist government came to power in Iran through a violent revolution in 1979. The revolution overthrew the brutal and repressive regime of the shah of Iran—whose government was supported by the United States—and replaced it with a theocratic government headed by Shiite Muslim religious leaders. The new government, led by the Ayatollah Ruhollah Khomeini, imposed a strict version of Islamic law on Iran. It required women to cover their hair in public, imposed a strict separation of the sexes almost everywhere, and restricted the movies and television shows the people of Iran could watch.

The people of Iran retained some freedom of choice after the revolution. Unlike some other Middle Eastern countries, the people of Iran elect a president and national legislature. Iranian women can vote, go to school, and hold jobs. However, the efforts of reformers to win more freedom have been stopped by conservative ayatollahs. Conversely, some ayatollahs have worked for greater freedom. However, most of the pressure for change in Iran comes from young people who are more open to new ideas from the outside world.

A bride and groom make their way to the mosque at Khiva in Uzbekistan. Social practices, such as the ceremonies surrounding weddings, vary widely throughout the Muslim world.

Views on Culture and Values

In its 2001–02 survey of the Islamic world, the Gallup Organization asked thousands of Muslims for their opinions about a wide variety of cultural practices and values. The following provides an overview of cultural practices that are common in the Islamic world, and explains what the Gallup Organization learned about the views of Muslims toward these practices.

LOVE AND MARRIAGE

Marriages are happy events for families in the Islamic world. Young Muslim men and women may choose to marry after meeting socially and falling in love, but the traditional arranged marriage, in which the parents choose who their children will marry, still occurs in some rural areas. Islamic law decrees the young couple must agree to the match.

Even when a young Muslim meets a potential marriage partner, there are strict rules regulating the time they can spend together. Western-style dating is particularly rare in rural areas; instead, young single men and women often meet in a group setting, then ask their families to help them find out more about a person that interests them. In cosmopolitan urban centers, like Cairo, Damascus, or Beirut, men and women who are engaged will often go out together, although they are supposed to stay in public places in order to avoid the temptation of premarital sex. Nevertheless, like all societies in the world, premarital sex does take place, although it is not as common as in the West.

Before a couple is married, the families of the bride and groom often negotiate a marriage contract that may include a payment of money or valuables to the bride called a *mahr* (dowry). The bride either saves the dowry as financial security for herself, or she may spend the dowry on helping to prepare the marital home. Islamic law, however, strongly recommends that the bride not spend the dowry on preparing the marital home and forbids the family of the bride from taking the dowry or spending it on themselves. (In practice this restriction is often violated, especially in poor countries.)

Some Muslims may marry early in life—in Iran young men can be married at age fourteen and girls at age nine.

Nearly all Muslim weddings are large affairs that involve many people and can last for days. In many Muslim communities, the newlyweds hold an elaborate feast that may last up to a week. The extended families of both bride and groom attend, and local poor people are often invited to share in the feast as well. The bride, and sometimes also the groom, will usually dress in rich, colorful clothes.

The wide variety of Muslim wedding traditions throughout the world reflects the broad cultural differences in the Islamic world.

Celebrations often follow local customs that may predate Islam. In countries like Malaysia or Afghanistan, the couple sits on thrones and is treated like royalty on their wedding day. Before many Muslim weddings, a temporary dye called henna is painted in elaborate designs on the hands of the bride and groom. Some Muslims in Sudan celebrate a marriage with races, contests, and dancing with swords. In the United Arab Emirates, the bride stays at home and has no visitors for 40 days before the wedding day, when she is covered from head to toe with perfumes and oils. A bride in Palestine may wear a headdress made from hundreds of coins. A newly married husband in Yemen follows an old wedding tradition when he tries to step on his wife's foot as they enter their house. If he succeeds, it is considered a sign that he will rule the house. If she pulls her foot away in time, she will be the boss.

Polygamy (the practice of a man taking more than one wife) is rare in the modern Islamic world, and several countries, such as Tunisia, have outlawed the practice. Some scholars of the Qur'an have argued that the practice was accepted at the time of Muhammad's revelations because it was very widespread on the Arabian Peninsula, but they point out that the Qur'an treats the

Muslim brides are often painted with henna in intricate patterns before their wedding day.

practice of polygamy with skepticism, if not outright hostility. In the Arab society of Muhammad's day, warriors often died young, leaving behind young widows who would not be cared for unless they remarried. Qur'an 4: 3 amended an existing custom that allowed men to take unlimited wives; Muslims were permitted four wives, but only if the man could afford to care for each of them equally. In the modern era, some Muslims have proposed that Qur'an 4: 129—which reads in part, "You are never able to be fair and just between women even if that were your ardent desire"—supports monogamy.

The 2001 Gallup Poll of the Islamic World asked people in Saudi Arabia, Kuwait, Jordan, and Lebanon about their views on love and marriage. Although the populations of each of these states are primarily Arab, the responses varied significantly.

When asked their attitudes on polygamy, a majority of the respondents said they do not support the practice. However, in the countries of the Arabian Peninsula there was a wide disparity between the answers of men and women. In Saudi Arabia, 47 percent of men support the practice while 72 percent of women disagree. In Kuwait 58 percent of men believe polygamy is acceptable, while 55 percent of women are opposed to the practice.

"The high level of Saudi women's disagreement with polygamy is especially noteworthy, given that the country is the spiritual heart of Islam and a society in which the role and conduct of women remains very strictly prescribed," notes Richard Burkholder, the Gallup Organization's director of international polling. "In Saudi Arabia, moral strictures require that all respondents in face-to-face, in-home interviews be polled by interviewers of the same gender. Ironically, this may have increased the willingness of women—and perhaps men as well—to candidly express their own feelings on this issue."

In Jordan and Lebanon, located near the eastern Mediterranean Sea, the practice is less acceptable. In Jordan, 61 percent of men and 80 percent of women are opposed to polygamy, while in Lebanon 80 percent of men and 91 percent of women disagree

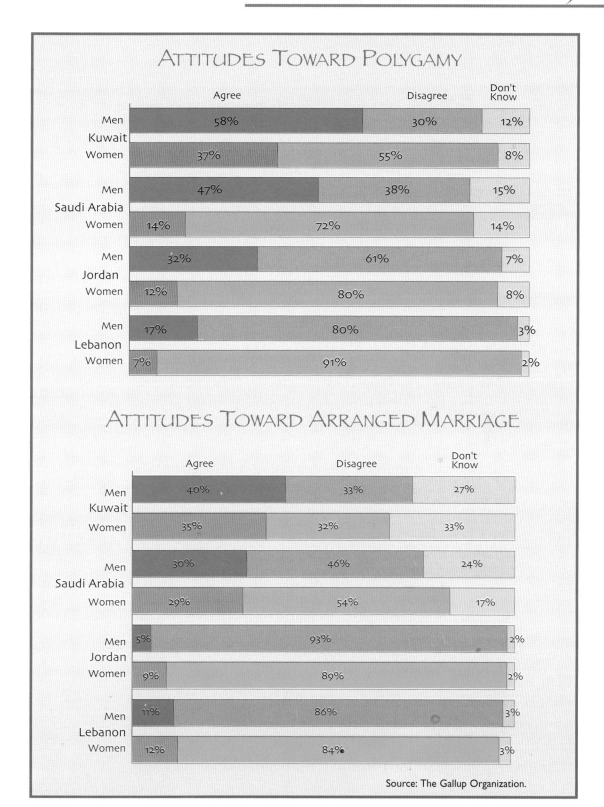

ATTITUDES TOWARD POLYGAMY

	Agree	Disagree	Don't Know
Kuwait Men	58%	30%	12%
Women	37%	55%	8%
Saudi Arabia Men	47%	38%	15%
Women	14%	72%	14%
Jordan Men	32%	61%	7%
Women	12%	80%	8%
Lebanon Men	17%	80%	3%
Women	7%	91%	2%

ATTITUDES TOWARD ARRANGED MARRIAGE

	Agree	Disagree	Don't Know
Kuwait Men	40%	33%	27%
Women	35%	32%	33%
Saudi Arabia Men	30%	46%	24%
Women	29%	54%	17%
Jordan Men	5%	93%	2%
Women	9%	89%	2%
Lebanon Men	11%	86%	3%
Women	12%	84%	3%

Source: The Gallup Organization.

with the practice. The population of Lebanon is unique among Arab states because of its high Christian population—about one-third of the population is Christian. About 93 percent of Lebanese Christians disagreed with the practice of polygamy, while 80 percent of the Muslims opposed the practice.

Attitudes about the practice of arranged marriages vary widely. In Kuwait, 40 percent of men and 35 percent of women agree with the practice, while 33 percent of men and 32 percent of women disagree. (The remaining 27 percent of men and 33 percent of women were either unsure or did not answer.) By contrast, in Jordan just 5 percent of men and 9 percent of women agreed with the practice, while 93 percent of men and 89 percent of women disagreed. (Just 2 percent were unsure or did not answer.)

RAISING A FAMILY

The married couple will soon turn to having children. Islamic law permits them to use birth control to limit the number of children they have. However, a large family is valued in many Muslim societies.

A newborn baby quickly receives an initiation into Islam. As soon as the umbilical cord is cut, many Muslims follow a tradition of whispering the Muslim call to prayer—the same words the child will hear from the local mosque five times each day—in each ear. Other parents whisper other things, such as the first chapter of the Qur'an. To give thanks for the birth, the parents may also follow an old Arab custom of shaving the baby's head and giving the poor an amount of gold or silver equal to the weight of the hair. A sheep or other animal is sometimes slaughtered and eaten in celebration of the birth.

The parents name the baby between seven and forty days after birth in a ceremony with relatives and friends. Islamic law provides guidelines for parents in choosing names, which all have meanings. A name may describe a positive quality about the child, or express the wishes of the parent for the child. Parents may also name their children after Muhammad or other prophets or heroes of Islamic history. The name cannot be tasteless, offensive, or indicate that the child serves anyone other than Allah. Some common Arabic names for boys include "Abd Allah" ("servant of Allah"), "Ali" ("excellent"), and "Karim" ("generous"). Some popular girls' names include "Fatima" (this was the name of a daughter of Muhammad), "Nawal" ("gift"), and "Iman" ("faith").

A child born to Muslim parents will learn about his or her religion on a daily basis. Among the first words taught to many children are, "In the name of Allah, the Merciful, the Compassionate." With these words, Muslims affirm their connection to Allah in their daily lives. Children see their parents praying and join in the prayers after learning how they are performed. Parents are responsible for ensuring that their children understand their religion, in addition to teaching them manners and proper behavior.

A Sunni Muslim and his son lift their hands during a service at a mosque. Children are taught about their religion from an early age.

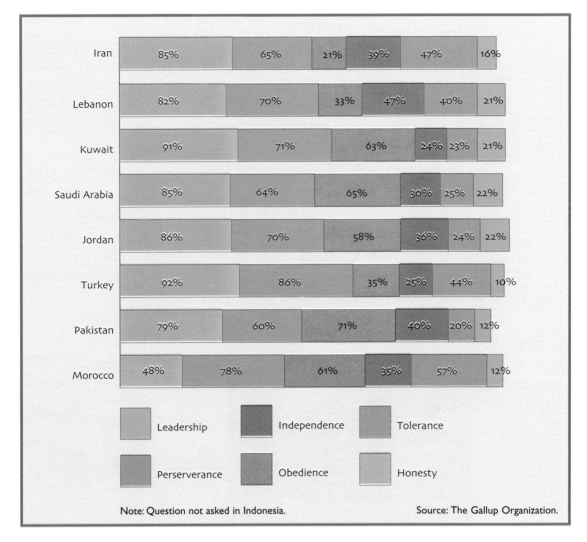

| | Iran | Lebanon | Kuwait | Saudi Arabia | Jordan | Turkey | Pakistan | Morocco |

Iran: 85% 65% 21% 39% 47% 16%

Lebanon: 82% 70% 33% 47% 40% 21%

Kuwait: 91% 71% 63% 24% 23% 21%

Saudi Arabia: 85% 64% 65% 30% 25% 22%

Jordan: 86% 70% 58% 36% 24% 22%

Turkey: 92% 86% 35% 25% 44% 10%

Pakistan: 79% 60% 71% 40% 20% 12%

Morocco: 48% 78% 61% 35% 57% 12%

Leadership   Independence   Tolerance

Perserverance   Obedience   Honesty

Note: Question not asked in Indonesia.   Source: The Gallup Organization.

The Gallup Organization asked respondents, "Here is a list of qualities which children can be encouraged to learn at home. Which three do you consider to be most important?" The figures here reflect the percent who mentioned each quality. (The total is more than 100 percent because each person could give three answers.)

Islam places a high value on children respecting their parents and honoring them by growing up to be honest and decent adults. Muslim children are taught to speak politely to their elders and help with household chores or duties. In some cultures children are expected to stand when their parents enter a room.

In the Islamic world, when a person reaches puberty he or she is considered an adult. Adulthood brings additional responsibilities for proper behavior, and the young adults are held accountable for their actions. Adult Muslims are expected to care for aging parents. Even after a parents' death, some Muslims may feel an obligation to fulfill promises their parents made. They may even go on the *hajj* to Mecca for their mother or father if either parent did not go before dying.

According to the Gallup poll of the Islamic world, many Muslims feel that honesty and tolerance are the two most important qualities they can teach their children at home. When given a list of seven qualities—honesty, tolerance, obedience, independence, perseverance, leadership, and imagination—and asked which three were the most important, between 82 percent and 92 percent of people in Lebanon, Kuwait, Saudi Arabia, Jordan, Turkey, Pakistan, and Iran selected honesty. Tolerance was chosen by between 60 percent and 86 percent of people in those seven countries plus Morocco. (The question was not asked in Indonesia.)

Perseverance and independence seemed to be valued about the same. Between 24 and 47 percent of the people in the eight countries where the question was asked selected independence as an important quality, compared to a range of 23 to 57 percent for perseverance. Leadership and imagination were the least valued qualities. The most controversial quality was obedience, as the percentage of people who listed it in the top three ranged from 71 percent in Pakistan to 21 percent in Iran.

The Gallup Organization found that the importance of obedience was closely related to the respondents' levels of education. In all of the countries surveyed, people with higher education (secondary school or higher) were much less likely to rate obedience among the top three qualities than were people with a lower education (up to elementary school). The difference of opinion between the two educational groups was greater than 20 percentage points in Kuwait, Jordan, Pakistan, Morocco, and Turkey, and between 10 and 15 percentage points in Saudi Arabia, Lebanon, and Iran.

PERCENTAGE OF POPULATION WITH SECONDARY EDUCATION OR HIGHER

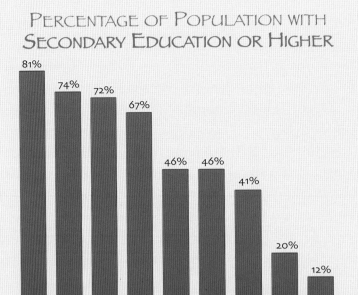

PERCENTAGE OF POPULATION WITH UNIVERSITY EDUCATION

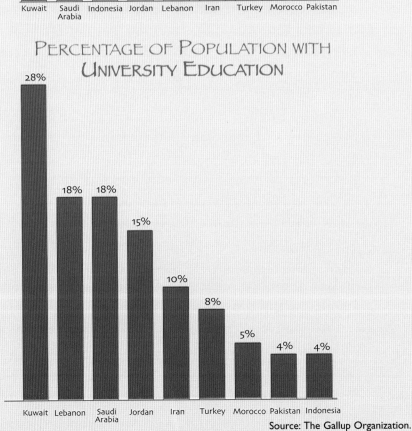

Source: The Gallup Organization.

EDUCATION IN THE ISLAMIC WORLD

Depending on where a child lives, he or she may attend a public school or an Islamic school, called a madrasa. In many countries, religious education is the core of learning. Boys and girls learn about the Qur'an even before they can read it. After Muslims learn to read, many will work for years to memorize the entire Qur'an. Because Muslims believe that the Qur'an can only be understood in Arabic, children who speak another language often learn Arabic in addition to their native language. When the child memorizes the entire Qur'an, the family may mark the event by inviting relatives and friends to a celebration, where the child will recite passages from memory. In their schools young Muslims also study the same subjects American students do—mathematics, science, history, art, and so on.

In the nine countries of the Islamic world surveyed by the Gallup Organization, levels of education vary greatly. Kuwait has the highest number of people achieving a secondary level of education, at 81 percent, followed by Saudi Arabia (74 percent), Indonesia (72 percent), and Jordan (67 percent). The lowest-ranking countries are Pakistan (12 percent) and Morocco (20 percent). In Pakistan, 36 percent of the population receives no formal education at all, followed by Morocco at 26 percent.

In the urban centers of the Islamic world, college education is becoming more common. In many Muslim countries colleges are free and public, so even in rural areas an increasing number of Muslims end up going to college. According to the Gallup Poll, among the nine countries studied Kuwait has the greatest percentage of people who complete studies at a college or university (28 percent), followed by Saudi Arabia and Lebanon (each at 18 percent). By comparison, data from the 2000 U.S. Census indicates that 15.5 percent of Americans had completed a college degree.

In many Islamic countries, men and women have equal opportunities to receive an education. In Kuwait, for example, 81 percent of men and 80 percent of women have completed a secondary level

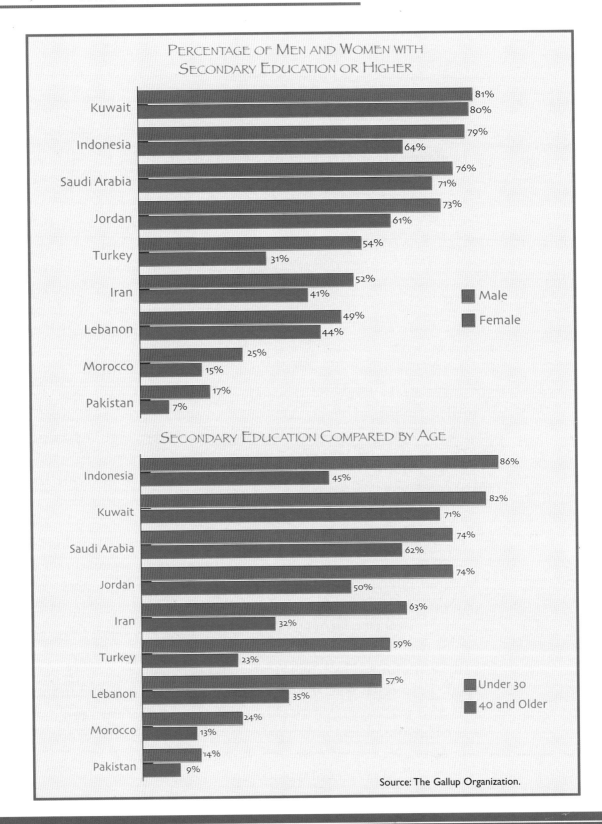

PERCENTAGE OF MEN AND WOMEN WITH
SECONDARY EDUCATION OR HIGHER

Kuwait — 81% / 80%
Indonesia — 79% / 64%
Saudi Arabia — 76% / 71%
Jordan — 73% / 61%
Turkey — 54% / 31%
Iran — 52% / 41%
Lebanon — 49% / 44%
Morocco — 25% / 15%
Pakistan — 17% / 7%

■ Male
■ Female

SECONDARY EDUCATION COMPARED BY AGE

Indonesia — 86% / 45%
Kuwait — 82% / 71%
Saudi Arabia — 74% / 62%
Jordan — 74% / 50%
Iran — 63% / 32%
Turkey — 59% / 23%
Lebanon — 57% / 35%
Morocco — 24% / 13%
Pakistan — 14% / 9%

■ Under 30
■ 40 and Older

Source: The Gallup Organization.

of education, while in Saudi Arabia the figures are 76 percent of men and 71 percent of women. Of the countries included in the Gallup Organization's survey, Turkey had the largest "gender gap" when it came to education (54 percent of men had completed at least a secondary level of education, compared to 31 percent of women). Women have great opportunities to receive an education in many other Islamic countries as well. Females make up 52 percent of the medical students in Egypt, and can be found in colleges and universities throughout the Islamic world.

The Gallup Organization also found that in the countries with the lowest educational levels, there are wide gaps between the percentages of men and women who receive no formal education. In Morocco, 41 percent of women report that they have not received any schooling, compared to 11 percent of men. The situation is similar in Pakistan, where 49 percent of women have no education, compared to 22 percent of men.

DIVORCE IN ISLAMIC SOCIETY

Divorce (*talaq*) is not taken lightly in Islamic law. In pre-Islamic Arabia men could divorce their wives at will, but in Islamic law a husband must declare his intention to divorce his wife three times to make it irrevocable. Qur'an 4: 35 first counsels arbitration when divorce is discussed. If this fails, the advisable course is for the husband to say "I divorce you" once and enter a three-month waiting period to see if the couple can reconcile and to make sure the wife is not pregnant. If the husband reconsiders, the couple can get back together. If they do not reconcile, and the husband utters the divorce declaration twice more, their divorce is final. In another approach, the husband makes the declaration of divorce once each month for three months. At any time during this three-month period, the couple can stop the divorce action, but at the end the divorce is irrevocable. The most frowned upon, and yet most common, type of divorce is the triple *talaq*, in which the husband utters the

A class of young girls practice reading the Qur'an in a school in the Banda Aceh province of Indonesia. According to the Gallup Organization's 2001–02 study, Indonesia has one of the best educational systems in the Islamic world.

divorce formula three times all at once.

Women can sue for divorce only on limited grounds, such as the impotence or insanity of her husband or for desertion or failure to support. Quite often, however, women do not exercise their right to divorce because, in many male-dominated societies, they are not informed about their legal rights. In recent years some Muslim countries have expanded their laws to give women more grounds for divorce and to provide women with more material compensation when their husbands divorce them. However, in other Muslim countries such as Pakistan, Nigeria, and Saudi Arabia, women are not treated fairly by matrimonial or criminal courts. This does not change the fact that doctrinally Islamic law is clear in its opposition to discrimination against women.

Wife beating occurs in some parts of the Islamic world, but it is not looked upon favorably. Many Muslim countries criminalize the behavior, and a husband can go to prison for a period ranging from six months to three years for assaulting his wife. Such prosecutions are common, especially in situations where there is a physical injury. In addition, one of the Hadith says, "The worst of men are those who beat their wives. [By doing so] they are no longer one of us." If wife beating occurs, neighbors and family usually intervene to stop the abuse, often reminding the offending husband of what the Prophet said about wife-beaters.

In recent years, the practice of stipulated divorces (known as *talaq al-tafwid*) has become more popular. The Prophet Muhammad sanctioned this practice during the early years of Islam, but there was much culture-based resistance. In these cases, a stipulation is entered into the marital contract dictating that if the husband commits certain conduct, the wife acquires an immediate right to a divorce. In effect, the stipulation acts as a prenuptial agreement that grants women considerable power within a marriage by challenging the traditionally exclusive male prerogative over divorce. In the modern age, a large number of women rekindled this practice by entering into prenuptial agreements granting wives the right to divorce their husbands, if the wives wish to do so.

When divorce occurs, children enter the custody of either the mother or the father depending on their age. In most instances, boys under the age of nine and girls under the age of 12 are given into the custody of the mother. Thereafter, custody reverts to the father.

The Gallup Organization asked residents of four Arab countries—Kuwait, Saudi Arabia, Jordan, and Lebanon—about their views on the moral admissibility of divorce. For this question, a

five-point scale was used, ranging from the view that divorce can
be completely justified (five) to the belief that divorce cannot be
justified at all (one).

In Jordan and Lebanon, more people hold the view that divorce
can never be justified than say that it can be completely justified.
In Jordan, 29 percent of men and 30 percent of women said that
divorce could not be justified at all, compared to 24 percent of
men and 21 percent of women who find the practice completely
justifiable. In Lebanon, the figures were 28 percent of men and 33
percent of women opposed to divorce, with 25 percent of men and

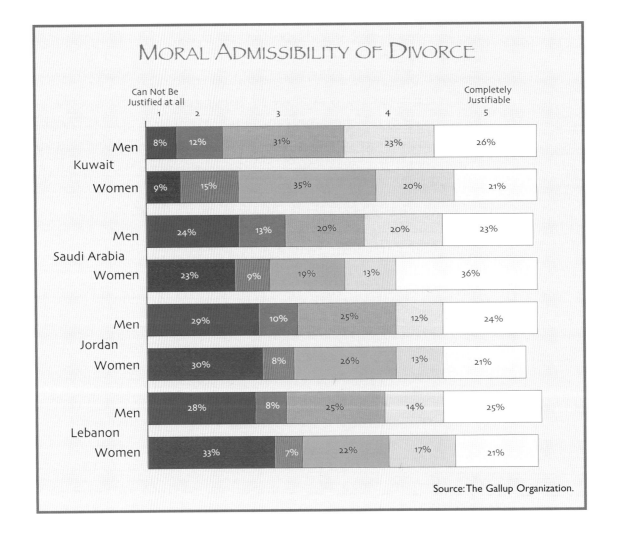

MORAL ADMISSIBILITY OF DIVORCE

Can Not Be
Justified at all

Completely
Justifiable

	1	2	3	4	5

Kuwait
Men: 8% | 12% | 31% | 23% | 26%
Women: 9% | 15% | 35% | 20% | 21%

Saudi Arabia
Men: 24% | 13% | 20% | 20% | 23%
Women: 23% | 9% | 19% | 13% | 36%

Jordan
Men: 29% | 10% | 25% | 12% | 24%
Women: 30% | 8% | 26% | 13% | 21%

Lebanon
Men: 28% | 8% | 25% | 14% | 25%
Women: 33% | 7% | 22% | 17% | 21%

Source: The Gallup Organization.

21 percent of women in support of the practice.

In the more conservative societies of Kuwait and Saudi Arabia, the reverse was true. In Saudi Arabia, 23 percent of men and 36 percent of women said that divorce was completely justifiable, compared to 24 percent of men and 23 percent of women who said divorce cannot be justified. In Kuwait, just 8 percent of men and 9 percent of women felt that divorce cannot be justified; 26 percent of men and 21 percent of women felt the practice was completely justifiable.

A group of Pakistanis, including women, wave signs picturing former premier Benazir Bhutto. The role of women in Islamic countries varies widely. In some places, such as Pakistan, women can be fully involved in public life. Other countries, such as Saudi Arabia, place greater restrictions on the role of women.

Women and Islam

Many westerners believe that the role of women in Muslim societies is one of the biggest differences between the Islamic world and the West. Images of Muslim women veiled from head to toe and stories about the persecution of women in the Islamic world circulate throughout the United States and other western countries. However, the status of women in Islamic countries is more complicated than the pictures and stereotypes common in the Western media. For example, no woman has ever been elected president or vice-president of the United States, but in 1989 a woman named Benazir Bhutto became the leader of Pakistan. Turkey, Bangladesh, and Indonesia have also chosen women as national leaders. Even in Iran, where a strict version of Islamic law is enforced, women can get jobs, go to college, run businesses, and vote in national elections. Egyptian women began a women's liberation movement at the beginning of the 20th century, before a similar movement emerged in the United States.

Although some people in the West condemn treatment of women in the Islamic world as unfair, westerners often forget that their own societies did not give women equal treatment until very recently. Before laws and attitudes changed during the 1960s and 1970s, women in the United States were commonly excluded from the best colleges and the best jobs, earned less pay than men for doing the same jobs, and had fewer rights to own property or borrow money. There are still Americans alive today who can remember when women were not allowed to vote—a right they won in 1920.

ISLAM'S TREATMENT OF WOMEN

Before the rise of Islam, women living on the Arabian Peninsula had few rights. The Arab societies of Muhammad's time were patriarchal, and men were the leaders of families and tribes. Women could not inherit money or property, and widows were considered the property of their deceased husband's family. *Polygyny*, or the practice of having multiple wives, was widespread, and men could marry or divorce at will.

It is important to keep in mind, however, that in most ancient societies women had few or no rights. In the Indus Valley civilizations, and in the ancient Greek and Roman empires, women were often considered to be possessions of their husbands. Women were even treated differently from men in the writings and teachings of early Jewish and Christian leaders.

Islam improved the status of women. The Prophet Muhammad taught that women had legal rights equal to those of men. The Qur'an gives women certain rights in marriage—they are no longer to be considered the property of their husbands—and says mothers deserve more respect from children than fathers do.

This drawing shows mercenaries transporting veiled female prisoners. Before the emergence of Islam in the seventh century, women were often considered property. The teachings of the Qur'an gave greater status and more rights to Muslim women.

Although Islamic law considers the most important duty of women to be their roles as wives, mothers, and homemakers, women are permitted to inherit property, manage their own money, and seek employment or own businesses. The Qur'an says that Muslims have a sacred duty to educate girls. Women participate in the religious duties of Islam, and can serve as religious leaders for other women. Muhammad expected women to fulfill different roles than men, but not necessarily unequal roles. In his final sermon the Prophet told his followers, "Treat your women well and be kind to them for they are your partners and committed helpers."

Before Muhammad's time, inheritance was passed only to men. The nearest male relative of the deceased received the inheritance, even if a female relative was more closely related. The fourth *sura* of the Qur'an granted women the right to inherit property. The Qur'an stipulates that wives, daughters, sisters, and mothers of the deceased are entitled to their share of the inheritance before the remainder is passed on the nearest male relative. In most cases, however, men were given twice the inheritance of women, the reasoning being that they were expected to bear financial responsibility for every member of their households.

Today, the treatment of women in the Islamic world varies from country to country, and depends as much on local customs and traditions as on religious views. In Turkey, Malaysia, and Indonesia, women have the same rights as men. Countries like Egypt have made steady advances in their treatment of women, and today women throughout the Islamic world have better access to education, health care, and jobs. At the other extreme, Saudi Arabia places some of the most severe restrictions on women. Women are banned from working in many professions, or even driving cars. They must get permission from their husband or father to do many other things, such as travel. Punishment for breaking the rules can be severe. And all women in Saudi Arabia—even non-Muslims—must veil themselves in public.

THE SEGREGATION OF WOMEN

In some Islamic societies, the veil is a powerful symbol of submission to Allah. Many Muslim women believe that to fulfill the Qur'an's requirement to dress modestly, they should cover their hair or even their entire face. Others veil themselves because it is the custom of their family or community. In Turkey, it is estimated that three-fourths of women wear the *hijab*, a head scarf that covers the hair and neck but leaves the face visible.

The veil is meant to protect women from unwanted attention from men, and some women want this protection. To many Muslim women, covering their hair and dressing modestly is a way to keep others from judging them by their appearance. A woman may also want to protect herself from the sun and dust— which is why men in some hot, dry regions wear a veil too.

In recent decades, women have donned veils to call for a return to Islamic values, or to protest against Western influence or corruption in their governments. Though veiling had been declining for some time in countries like Iraq, Syria, Lebanon, and Jordan, the practice has increased again. Ironically, as women are granted new freedoms to work and attend universities, the veil provides them with some protection from male harassment.

Some sociologists and anthropologists have argued that the practice of wearing a veil has become a means of expressing dissent and opposition to secular governments in the Islamic world, and to social pressures that demand greater levels of Westernization and that dilute the people's sense of an Islamic identity. By wearing a veil, these experts say, women reassert their Islamic identity in response to the strong forces of Westernization.

Two German women wear *burqas* to protest against a court ruling that could outlaw religious dress in Germany's public schools. In September 2003 Germany's highest court ruled that a regional state was wrong in banning a Muslim teacher from wearing a headscarf, but said that individual states could pass new laws against religious dress in the classroom.

Women who live in countries like Iran and Saudi Arabia have no choice but to veil themselves. Women forced to wear a *burqa* or *abaya*—garments that cover the head and entire body like a cape—suffer from the heat and inconvenience these types of garments cause. Women in such countries may face punishment from the authorities if they appear in public without the proper covering. However, the number of women forced to wear such garments are the minority in the Islamic world. Most Muslim women in Turkey, Lebanon, Tunisia, Morocco, Algeria, the former Soviet republics, and other Islamic countries wear either a simple scarf or no head covering at all.

The veil is one way that women may be segregated, or kept separate from men. In regions where women are required to cover themselves, they may also be restricted to separate areas in schools, restaurants, theatres, swimming pools, or gymnasiums. In places where rigid versions of Islam are enforced, women might have to visit certain public places only at special times, or may be banned from them altogether.

The Urdu word *purdah* ("seclusion") is equivalent to the Arabic word *hijab*. It broadly refers to the practice of secluding women in public through the various types of veiling. *Purdah* also refers more specifically to segregating the sexes by keeping women in seclusion at home behind a high wall, curtain, or screen. The latter type of seclusion is not practiced by many Muslims, but is particularly prevalent in India (where some Hindus also follow this practice).

REPRESSION AND TRADITION

Although Islamic law gives specific freedoms to Muslim women, some Islamic countries have passed laws that place tight restrictions on the behavior and activities of women, above and beyond what is required by Islam. A commonly cited example occurred in Afghanistan, where the conservative Taliban held power from 1996 to 2001.

The Taliban instituted harsh restrictions on Afghan women. All women had to wear the *burqa* any time they appeared in public, and there were stories of women being beaten or stoned for not having the proper attire. Women were not permitted to work, so female teachers, doctors, lawyers, artists, and writers were forced to give up their jobs. This meant the women were dependent on their husbands or male relatives for food and shelter. Women also were barred from receiving an education, could not leave their homes without being accompanied by a close male relative, and had to follow many other laws prohibiting various behavior. Punishments for breaking the long list of restrictions on women included imprisonment, public flogging, amputation of fingers or limbs, and death by stoning.

Leaders of the Taliban declared that these restrictions were necessary to return the country to a pure form of Islam. Most other Muslims, however, disagreed. For example, the Organization of the Islamic Conference, an international group composed of more than fifty Muslim countries, did not accept the Taliban's restriction on women and did not recognize the Taliban government or invite its representative to join the organization.

Other countries, such as Sudan and Nigeria, have adopted strict laws and punishments based on their interpretation of Islamic law. The constitution of Sudan, a large country in Africa, establishes *Sharia* as the basis for legislation. Lawbreakers may be stoned, whipped, or killed; for example, the sentence for armed robbery is the amputation of the right hand and left foot. In both Sudan and Nigeria, women have been sentenced to death for having premarital sex.

In some parts of Africa, young women may undergo a barbaric procedure known as female circumcision or female genital mutilation (FGM). This horrible practice involves cutting off parts of the genitals of young girls. Although this practice is associated with the Islamic world, it is not derived from Islam; FGM occurs mostly in African communities, including non-Muslim areas. FGM is not mentioned in Islamic law, and most Muslim authorities say it is forbidden. Still, tens of thousands of African girls undergo this cruel practice, usually without benefit of painkillers or clean instruments. Today many activists and international human-rights organizations are working to stamp out this practice.

Many westerners feel that Islamic countries should not tolerate repressive attitudes and traditions concerning women. "The way Islam has been practiced in most Muslim societies for centuries has left millions of Muslim women with battered, bodies, minds, and souls," wrote Riffat Hassan, a religion professor in the United States, in a 2002 *Time* magazine article.

Throughout the Islamic world women's rights activists are claiming new freedom and power in many countries, but their progress is slow. Reformers often face stiff resistance from conservative people in their country who have a strict view of Islam or fear that

These young African girls have been ritually circumcised, a brutal procedure that involves cutting off parts of their genitals when they reach the age of nine. This barbaric practice is not sanctioned by the Qur'an or Islamic law; instead it is a traditional practice in some parts of Africa.

changes for women will lead to unstable families or changes in other laws. Nevertheless, there have been many improvements in recent years. Bangladesh has increased the penalties for crimes against women, such as kidnapping and rape. Egypt has improved its divorce laws to help women; the government has also banned the practice of female circumcision. Morocco's legislature has set aside thirty seats for women. Women are permitted to vote and to run for election in many of the Arab Gulf states, such as Oman, Qatar, and Bahrain, just as they are in Indonesia and several other Muslim countries. In Turkey, a married man can no longer make important legal decisions without his wife's agreement.

Muslim women who have the right to choose how they practice their religion and live their lives usually view Islam as a refuge that gives them more freedom, not less. Consider the words of a young American woman who chose to become a Muslim:

> Islam gave me something that was lacking in my life. I used to get so depressed trying to conform to our crazy culture and its image of what a woman should be, the emphasis we put on looking good— the hair, the makeup, the clothes—and our hunger for material wealth. It left me feeling empty all the time.

To this woman, Islam offered better treatment than western society. Communities throughout the Islamic world are trying to eliminate the abuse of Muslim women while at the same time promoting and reinforcing the many benefits Islam gives to women.

The Dome of the Rock in Jerusalem is part of Al-Haram al-Sharif (the Noble Sanctuary), one of the three most important sites in Islam. The status of Jerusalem is an important aspect of the conflict between Israel and the Palestinians. U.S. involvement in this long-running dispute is a major source of tension between the Islamic world and the West.

Views on the Issue of Palestine

The story of the ongoing conflict between Israel and its neighbors in the Middle East could fill an entire book. But a basic understanding of the roots of this conflict, and the different perspectives of the two sides, is essential to understanding certain attitudes in the Islamic world today.

The Israeli-Palestinian issue is only one of many instances where U.S. foreign policy involvement in the Islamic world has angered and offended Muslims. Examples include the United States's support for harsh regimes in Iran and Indonesia during the 1960s and 1970s; its involvement in Afghanistan in the 1980s and the U.S. overthrow of that country's Taliban government in 2001; and the U.S. invasion of Iraq in the spring of 2003 to overthrow the regime of Saddam Hussein. However, Palestine remains a critical issue in disagreements between Muslims and the West. Many Muslims feel that the U.S. supports Israel at the expense of the Palestinians, and consider the United States a puppet of Israel.

THE ROOT OF THE CONFLICT

Judaism is the oldest monotheistic faith, dating back to the time of the patriarch Abraham (about 1900 B.C.E.). In ancient times the Jews (then called Hebrews or Israelites) invaded the territory on the eastern Mediterranean coast, on the western side of the Jordan River (at the time this land was called Canaan). Over a long period of time the Hebrews fought with the other tribes who lived in Canaan, and they eventually established a rich Hebrew civilization. The high point of this civilization occurred around 1000 B.C.E., when King David established a powerful kingdom with its capital in Jerusalem. His son, Solomon, was a wise ruler who is credited with building a magnificent temple in Jerusalem. After Solomon's death, however, the Hebrew state split into a northern kingdom (Israel) and a southern kingdom (Judah). These smaller states were weakened by conflict with strong empires from Egypt and Mesopotamia. In 722 B.C.E. the Assyrians conquered the kingdom of Israel and carried off the Hebrews living there. The Babylonians conquered Jerusalem and destroyed the southern kingdom, Judah, in 586 B.C.E.; many Jews were taken to Babylon as captives.

After the Medes and Persians destroyed Babylon around 538 B.C.E., some Jews returned to Jerusalem, where they rebuilt their temple. However, the Jews were subject first to Persian rule and—after the armies of Alexander the Great conquered the Persians—to Hellenistic control. Around 165 B.C.E. the Maccabaean Revolt won the Jews their freedom from the Greek Seleucid rulers. Judea, as this new Jewish state was known, managed to remain independent until about 67 B.C.E., when it became part of the growing Roman Empire.

Some Jews did not like being a vassal state of Rome, and con-

A curving road runs through a valley in the Galilee region of Israel. The ancient Israelites established a strong kingdom in this area more than 3,000 years ago, under the rule of King David.

tinued fighting for their freedom from imperial rule. After a rebellion from C.E. 66–70, the Romans destroyed the Jewish temple; when another rebellion was put down around C.E. 133, the Romans forced many Jews to leave Judea and move to other parts of the empire. After this the Romans officially changed the name of the area to Palestine—the name by which it is often called today.

For thousands of years Jewish communities existed throughout Europe, North Africa, and the Middle East. Members of these communities often thrived, but Jews were also the victims of persecution at various times in history, particularly in Europe. Christian leaders often encouraged people to kill or forcibly convert Jews. (In general, the Jewish communities that existed in

Muslim lands—including small settlements in Palestine—were often safer from violence than those in Europe.)

During the late 1800s a new wave of harsh persecutions in eastern Europe, and the growing movement of nationalism, led some Jewish leaders to call for an independent Jewish state. This idea was called *Zionism*, after the hill named Zion where the ancient Jewish temple in Jerusalem once stood. Zionists began buying land in Palestine, particularly near Jerusalem. Initially, Palestinian

Four Allied leaders—David Lloyd George of Great Britain, Signor Orlando of Italy, Georges Clemenceau of France, and Woodrow Wilson of the United States—meet outside a hotel at the Paris Peace Conference, May 1919. Decisions made at this conference, which was held after an armistice ended the First World War, reshaped the world. Britain and France, in particular, were given a great deal of control over newly created countries in the Middle East, such as Syria, Lebanon, and Iraq. The British were granted control over the area historically known as Palestine.

Arabs welcomed the new settlers, but as the Jews took over more land the Muslim Arabs began to resist, and incidents of armed violence broke out between the two groups.

At this time Palestine was controlled by the Ottoman Empire. When World War I broke out Great Britain and its allies wanted to capture the strategically important territory. The British encouraged Arabs to revolt against Ottoman rule, and promised an influential Meccan leader named Sharif Hussein bin Ali that Great Britain would support an independent Arab state, under his control, if the Arabs successfully revolted. This some Arabs did in 1916.

At the same time, however, British Foreign Secretary Arthur James Lord Balfour sent a letter to Lord Rothschild, a Zionist leader, that contained the following statement: "His Majesty's Government view with favour the establishment in Palestine of a national home for the Jewish people, and will use their best endeavours to facilitate the achievement of this object, it being clearly understood that nothing shall be done which may prejudice the civil and religious rights of existing non-Jewish communities in Palestine, or the rights and political status enjoyed by Jews in any other country." The 1917 Balfour Declaration, as it became known, was intended to enlist Jewish support for the British war effort against Germany and its allies, but it was seen by Zionists as the first official recognition of their political aims.

Even before the British made these promises to the Arabs and Jews, they had already made plans to incorporate Palestine and other territories into their empire. In 1916 the British and French had secretly agreed to a plan to divide up the Ottoman territories in the Middle East. The Sykes-Picot Agreement separated the region into British and French spheres of influence.

In the peace conferences that followed the end of World War I, the League of Nations broke up the former Ottoman territories into new states such as Iraq, Syria, Lebanon, and Transjordan. The British received a League of Nations mandate to oversee Palestine. Under the mandate system, the British were supposed to prepare the newly formed countries for eventual independence; however, the new Arab states were little more than colonial dependencies.

Jewish immigration to Palestine continued during the 1920s and 1930s, particularly after the rise to power of Adolf Hitler's Nazi Party in Germany. As the Nazis stepped up their persecution of German Jews, thousands of refugees fled to Palestine. The continuing influx of Jewish immigrants led to continued violence between Jews and Arabs, while both sides fought the continued British presence in the land.

In 1939, with the Arabs revolting against British rule and with Europe about to plunge into World War II, the British government issued a policy statement, called the White Paper of 1939, that limited Jewish immigration to Palestine. By 1941 the Nazis occupied most of Europe, and continued British enforcement of the immigration quotas meant European Jews had no place to go in order to escape Hitler's "final solution"—his plan to exterminate the Jews of Europe. As a result, some 6 million Jews died in Nazi concentration camps.

THE ESTABLISHMENT OF ISRAEL

After the end of World War II, the Zionists increased their efforts to create a Jewish state in Palestine. However, the Arab majority of Palestine was opposed. The newly formed United Nations stepped in, unveiling a plan in 1947 to divide Palestine into two countries—one Jewish and one Arab—with Jerusalem, considered a holy city by both Jews and Muslims as well as Christians, to be open to everyone under U.N. administration. Neither side liked this plan, but Jewish leaders in Palestine agreed to the partition.

While the issue was still undecided, Britain announced that it would withdraw from Palestine on May 14, 1948. At midnight May 15, the Jewish leaders declared the formation of the independent state of Israel, within the boundaries delineated by the United Nations' partition plan. Immediately, troops of five neighboring Arab countries, which had never agreed to the plan, attacked Israel. In fierce fighting over the next two years Israel defeated the Arab armies, winning its independence.

Owing to the 1948–49 war, tens of thousands of Palestinian Arabs had fled their homes, hoping to avoid violence, terrorism, and war. By the end of the war, it is estimated that between 500,000 and 750,000 Palestinians had left their homes. Some moved during the fighting to the West Bank or Gaza Strip—territories that had been seized by Jordan and Egypt, respectively. Other Palestinians ended up in hastily built refugee camps in Lebanon, Syria, or Jordan.

Occasional fighting between Israel and its neighbors continued throughout the 1950s and early 1960s. The Arab countries refused to recognize the right of Israel to exist. In June 1967, Israel feared that Egypt, Syria, and other Arab countries were preparing an attack, so it launched a pre-emptive strike against its neighbors. The surprise attack was successful, and in less than a week Israeli forces had seized a huge area of territory, including East Jerusalem and the West Bank from Jordan, the Gaza Strip and Sinai Peninsula from Egypt, and the Golan Heights from Syria.

The June 1967 War led another wave of Palestinian Arabs to leave their homes and flee to the refugee camps outside of Israel. At the same time, the Israeli occupation of East Jerusalem, the West Bank, and the Gaza Strip placed more than a million Palestinian Arabs under the control of Israel's government. Israeli troops enforced martial law throughout the occupied territories, and Palestinians were permitted few rights in Israeli society. The Israeli government also took over ownership of property left behind by Palestinian refugees, distributing the land to Jewish settlers.

Until 1967, many Palestinian Arabs—both refugees and those living in the occupied territories—had hoped that the other Arab states would help them to regain their lands by conquering Israel. After the June 1967 War it was obvious that Israel was much stronger militarily than its Arab neighbors. Although there had been Palestinian opposition groups before the war, they began to attract new followers and become more radical. Organizations like the Palestine Liberation Organization (PLO) were soon attacking

Israeli targets. Israel retaliated by bombing PLO bases in Lebanon and Jordan and assassinating suspected Palestinian leaders.

THE U.S. BECOMES INVOLVED

The United States has had a long relationship with Israel, and is considered one of the Jewish state's strongest supporters. But even though the U.S. had been the first country to officially recognize the state of Israel in 1948, a close relationship did not develop until after the June 1967 War. This was in part because of the ongoing Cold War, which pitted the U.S. against the Soviet Union. U.S. policymakers feared that supporting Israel would cause the Arab states to side with the U.S.S.R., and shift the balance of power in the strategic oil-rich Middle East.

By 1967, however, Egypt and other Arab states were already receiving weapons and aid from the Soviet Union. When Israel proved that, compared to the Arab countries, it was a strong military power, U.S. policymakers felt that the best way to contain the spread of communism in the Middle East was to keep Israel stronger than its Arab neighbors. Since the June 1967 War the U.S. has been Israel's main supplier of military weapons and training. Israel is also the largest recipient of U.S. financial assistance; today the country receives about $3 billion each year.

The United States has tried to help Israel make peace with its neighbors. In 1977 U.S. President Jimmy Carter helped negotiate a peace treaty between Israel and Egypt, the largest and strongest Arab state. In return for peace, Israel agreed to give up the Sinai Peninsula territory it had occupied since the June 1967 War. The peace treaty was widely praised in the West. However, many Arabs were angered by it, because this separate peace treaty that Egypt made with Israel left other Arab states in a much weaker bargaining position. Egypt was ejected from the Arab League and a Muslim extremist assassinated Egyptian president Anwar Sadat in 1982.

Although the land-for-peace trade went smoothly—Israel withdrew from the Sinai completely by 1982—there was a second part of the agreement that was never implemented. The agreement included a framework for negotiations to eventually create an autonomous state for Palestinian Arabs in the West Bank and Gaza Strip. This section of the treaty was vaguely worded, however, and no progress was made toward establishing a Palestinian state.

The Palestinian Arab minority (consisting of Christians and Muslims) that live in Israel did not have the same freedom and opportunities as did Jewish citizens. Palestinians were not allowed to build mosques without permission from the government. They also saw a disparity in funding for education and medical services between Jewish and Arab neighborhoods. When it came to land disputes, Palestinians felt that Israeli courts favored Jewish new-comers and recent immigrants to Israel over Arab families that had established a long history in the land. Also, few Arabs were able to reach high-level governmental positions.

By the mid-1980s, Palestinian anger at the lack of progress, and at their oppressive living conditions, began to boil over. In 1987 a series of protests began in Gaza and the West Bank. This uprising

Egyptian president Anwar Sadat, U.S president Jimmy Carter, and Israeli prime minister Menachem Begin sign the Camp David Accords in September 1978. The agreement provided for a peace treaty between Israel and Egypt, which was signed in 1979, but it angered many people in the Muslim world.

became known as the *intifada*. Israeli troops responded with force to stone-throwing demonstrations by angry Palestinian civilians. According to B'Tselem, an Israeli human-rights group, more than 1,100 Palestinians and about 100 Israeli civilians were killed between 1987 and 1993.

At the end of the 1991 Gulf War, U.S. and Soviet leaders invited Israeli and Arab leaders to a conference in Madrid, Spain. The Madrid Conference ultimately led to Israel's signing a peace agreement with a second Arab state, Jordan, in 1994. It also contributed to a breakthrough in Israeli-Palestinian talks. After secret negotiations in Oslo, Norway, in 1993 Israel agreed to gradually permit limited Palestinian self-government in the occupied territories and to continue negotiations aimed at further satisfying the concerns of both parties. In September 1993, an agreement known as the Declaration of Principles was signed on the White House lawn, and sealed with a historic handshake between Israeli prime minister Yitzhak Rabin and PLO leader Yasir Arafat.

Over the next few years some progress was made toward a permanent solution to the Israeli-Palestinian problem. A provisional government, the Palestinian Authority, was formed in 1994, and the next year Israel gave the authority control over parts of the West Bank. However, extremists on both sides made a fair peace settlement difficult. In Israel, orthodox Jews were angry about the country's surrender of territory; an Israeli militant assassinated Rabin in November 1995. After Benjamin Netanyahu, an opponent of the peace process, was elected prime minister in May 1996, he angered Muslims by authorizing an archaeological dig under al-Aqsa mosque, one of the holiest Islamic sites. On the Palestinian side, Arafat's efforts to maintain order were undercut by a devastating campaign of suicide bombings against both the Israeli military and civilians. The attacks, by the militant organization Hamas, further poisoned the prospects for peace.

U.S. President Bill Clinton pressured both Israelis and Palestinians to keep moving forward with the peace process, despite accusations by both sides that the other was not complying with the 1993

Declaration of Principles. In 1998 Netanyahu turned over control of more territory to the Palestinian Authority. However, in 1999 a five-year deadline for Palestinian statehood, which had been set in the original Oslo Accords, passed without the two sides agreeing on the most important issues—the borders of the Palestinian state, the status of East Jerusalem, and the right of Palestinian refugees to return to their homes in Israel. Arafat threatened to declare statehood unilaterally, but Clinton persuaded him to wait until an agreement could be reached with Israel. In July 2000 Clinton hosted a summit at Camp David between Arafat and Israeli prime minister Ehud Barak, who had been elected on a promise to create a lasting peace with the Palestinians. The talks failed.

The Palestinians were tired of waiting. In September of that year a second Palestinian *intifada* began in the occupied territories. Suicide bombing attacks by Palestinians became more common. Israel responded by replacing Palestinian self-rule with martial law, restricting Palestinian freedoms, and retaliating against suicide attacks with military force. The prospect for peace vanished beneath new waves of terror and repression.

In the West, Yasir Arafat received most of the blame for the collapse of the peace process. News reports painted Arafat as stubborn and not committed to peace, saying that Barak had offered "99 percent" of what the Palestinians had been asking for. Clinton himself said that Arafat was the reason the summit had failed. Arafat was also blamed for not doing enough to stop the violence of the second intifada.

People in the Islamic world saw the failure of the peace process differently. They felt that Clinton, who was supposed to be an impartial facilitator to the peace process during the 1990s, had instead sided with the Israelis, giving in to their demands while trying to wring greater concessions from Arafat. From the Palestinian point of view, Barak's proposal at Camp David did not fairly address the most important issues, such as the right of Palestinian refugees to return to their homes in Israel or receive compensation for their property. Also, the territory that Israel was prepared to concede was less than Palestinians felt they had been promised in the past. In the end, Arafat and the Palestinians felt that they had been betrayed both by Israel, which had not lived up to its Oslo promises, and by the United States, which had not made Israel meet its commitments.

Palestinians often point to the continued growth of Jewish settlements in the occupied territories as a sign that Israel had not acted in good faith during the peace process. In 1990, there had been approximately 76,000 Israeli settlers in some 150 settlements. By 2000, the population of Israeli settlements had increased to more than 200,000. Although Clinton called the settlements "obstacles to peace," he never used his leverage with the Israelis to stop their construction and expansion.

In 2003, U.S. President George W. Bush attempted to broker a new peace agreement between Israel and the Palestinians. The Bush administration's plan—often dubbed the "road map for peace"—called for the Palestinians to crack down on terrorism, Israel to dismantle settlements in the occupied territories, and for a Palestinian state to be established in the West Bank and Gaza Strip by the end of 2005. However, from the start it seemed unlikely that this optimistic deadline could be met.

MUSLIM VIEWS ON PALESTINE AND THE U.S.

The Israeli occupation of Palestinian lands has angered and frustrated many Muslims throughout the Islamic world—particularly Arabs. Most Muslims feel a kinship with the Palestinians, and believe they have been mistreated by Israel. Muslims also believe that Israel has unlawfully annexed Jerusalem, one of the most important cities in Islam. Muslims are not willing to concede control of Jerusalem to the Israelis. A result of this is that Muslims are angry at the United States because of its close ties to Israel and its financial and military support for the Jewish state.

In its survey of the Islamic World, the Gallup Organization captured the importance of Palestine to Muslims' opinion of the United States. Of the thousands of people polled, only 3 percent said that the United States's approach to the situation in Palestine is fair.

Although the Israeli-Palestinian situation is followed in all nine Muslim countries surveyed by the Gallup Organization, Arabs were most likely to pay close attention to news about Palestine. More than 84 percent of respondents in Jordan, Kuwait, Morocco, and Saudi Arabia said that they pay attention to news about Palestine. By contrast, interest is lower in the Muslim, but non-Arab, states Turkey (41 percent say news about Palestine attracts their attention), Pakistan (34 percent), Iran (27 percent), and Indonesia (16 percent).

Citizens in the nine Islamic countries surveyed are skeptical about the neutrality of the Western world in its handling of the Israeli-Palestinian conflict. The Gallup Organization asked respondents whether each of 10 positive attributes applied to Western nations. The attribute "fair in their stance toward the situation in Palestine" was the item least likely to be associated with the West in the Arab countries, Pakistan, and Turkey, and was among the lowest-ranked in Iran and Indonesia.

"[T]he perception that Western nations are not fair in their stances toward Palestine fits in with a more generalized view that the West is unfair to the Arab and Islamic worlds," notes Senior Gallup Poll Editor Lydia Saad. "What is not clear is whether the Palestinian issue drives these concerns, or whether it is just one of several examples of Western bias that might extend to Afghanistan, Iraq, Gulf oil, and other situations."

There seems to be a correlation between the attention that Muslims pay to news about Palestine and their personal impression of the United States and other Western nations. In most of the nine countries surveyed, respondents who pay close attention to the news about Palestine have a lower opinion of the United States than do respondents who pay less close attention. In Lebanon, for example, 51 percent of the people who said they pay close attention to news about Palestine have an unfavorable opinion of the

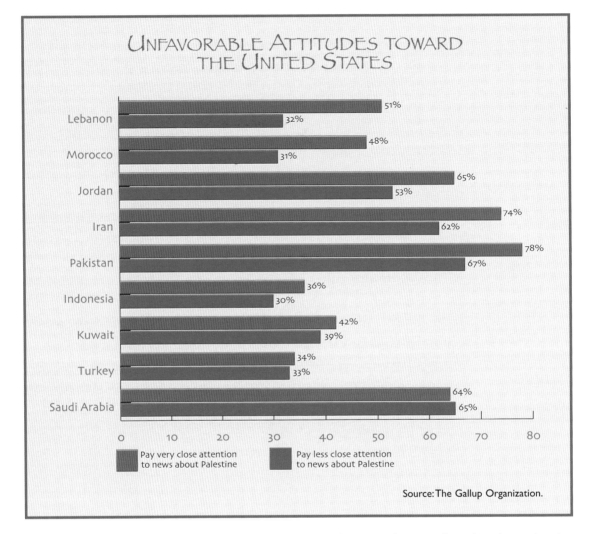

UNFAVORABLE ATTITUDES TOWARD THE UNITED STATES

Lebanon — 51% / 32%
Morocco — 48% / 31%
Jordan — 65% / 53%
Iran — 74% / 62%
Pakistan — 78% / 67%
Indonesia — 36% / 30%
Kuwait — 42% / 39%
Turkey — 34% / 33%
Saudi Arabia — 64% / 65%

Pay very close attention to news about Palestine

Pay less close attention to news about Palestine

Source: The Gallup Organization.

This chart reflects the difference in attitudes toward the United States, based on how closely people in the Islamic world follow news in Palestine. The poll asked, "Is your opinion of the United States very favorable, somewhat favorable, somewhat unfavorable, or very unfavorable." The percentages shown are the total that answered either "very unfavorable" or "somewhat unfavorable."

United States, compared to 32 percent unfavorable among those who do not pay close attention to the issue—a 19-point difference. The difference was 17 points in Morocco (48 percent to 31 percent), 12 points in Jordan (65 percent to 53 percent) and Iran (74 percent to 62 percent), 11 points in Pakistan (78 percent to 67 percent) and 6 points in Indonesia (36 percent to 30 percent).

"Overall, Gallup sees statistically significant increases in negative attitudes toward the United States according to respondents' attentiveness to the Palestine issue," said Lydia Saad. "This would suggest that the Palestinian issue is an important driver of negative attitudes toward the United States."

However, the Gallup Organization also noted that the U.S. attack on Afghanistan in the fall of 2001, undertaken to overthrow the Taliban government for harboring Osama bin Laden and his al-Qaeda network, caused a similar negative impact on Muslim views of the West. "This would support the idea that the Islamic world has multiple grievances toward the United States's foreign policy toward the Arab/Islamic worlds that jointly contributed to negative attitudes toward the United States," said Saad.

It is important to note that the Gallup survey was done before the United States invaded Iraq in March 2003. The war, and subsequent U.S. occupation of Iraq, has done even greater damage to the image of the United States in the Islamic world. It is quite possible that, if the study were redone today, the negative views of the United States would be even higher.

The conflict between Israel and Palestine continues to strain relations between the United States and many Arab and Islamic countries. Although many people in the United States would like to see a fair settlement of the issue, the decades of fighting combined with distrust of American motives and actions make that task extremely difficult.

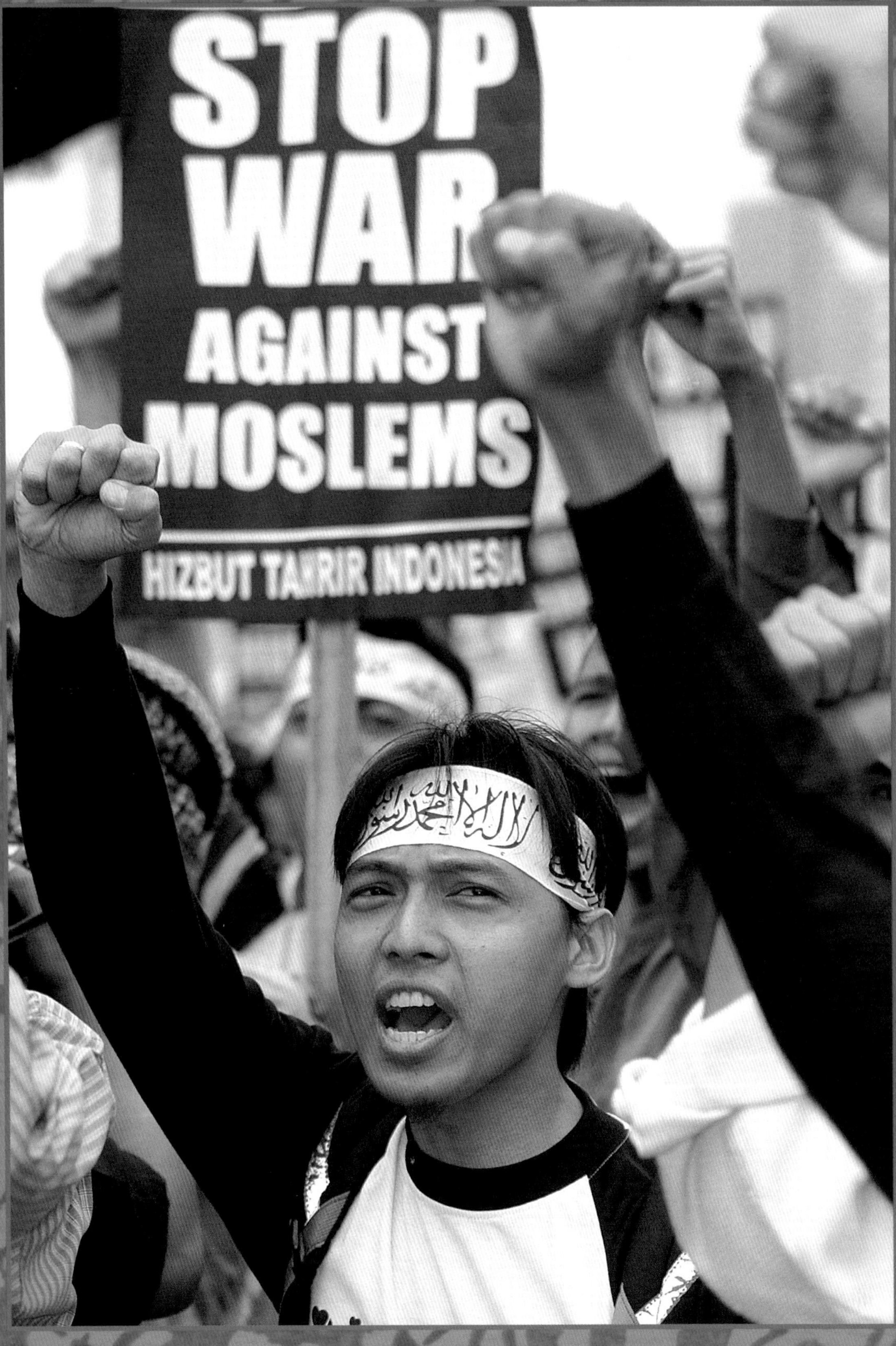
STOP
WAR
AGAINST
MOSLEMS
HIZBUT TAHRIR INDONESIA

Indonesian Muslims demonstrate outside the U.S. embassy in Jakarta to protest against the looming war against Iraq, January 2003. Many people in the Islamic world have unfavorable views of the United States, particularly in its attitude toward Muslim nations.

Views of the United States on Other Issues

In general, people who live in the United States feel that their country defends freedom and democracy, and that the U.S. gives generously to less-fortunate nations. Most U.S. citizens are likely to view their society as trustworthy, friendly, and compassionate toward poorer nations. By contrast, most of the people polled in the Gallup Organization's survey of the Islamic world have strongly unfavorable views of the United States and other Western nations.

"It is evident from the data reviewed in this project that the people of Islamic countries around the world have significant grievances with the West in general and with the United States in particular," says Gallup editor-in-chief Frank Newport. "At almost every opportunity within the survey, respondents overwhelmingly agree that the United States is aptly described by such negative labels as ruthless, aggressive, conceited, arrogant, easily provoked, biased. . . . The people of Islamic nations also believe that Western nations do not respect Arab or Islamic values, do not support Arabs causes, and do not exhibit fairness toward . . . Muslims."

The United States became deeply involved in world affairs after World War II, during a time of rising global tensions with the Union of Soviet Socialist Republics (U.S.S.R.). During this period, a major concern of U.S. foreign policy was to prevent the Soviet Union from expanding its influence. To achieve this, the U.S. and other western powers at times supported oppressive governments in Muslim countries and elsewhere because these governments opposed the Soviet Union and communism. In much of the Islamic world, Muslims still resent the U.S. for its foreign-policy actions during the past fifty years.

VIEWS ON WESTERN VALUES

The imposition of Western culture and values on the civilization of the Islamic world is a sore spot for many Muslims. People have argued that the influence of western values and exposure to western media, with its graphic depictions of violence, drug and alcohol abuse, and extramarital sex, undermines the culture of the Islamic world. Many people in the Islamic world agree over this matter, viewing the West as materialistic and indifferent to religious values. At the same time, however, they acknowledge the positive aspects of Western culture, such as advances in science and technology, and see western nations as educationally and economically advanced.

One question in the Gallup Organization's survey of the Islamic world asked, "How positively or negatively do you think our own value system is being influenced by the value system that prevails in the Western societies." Respondents were given a five-point scale, ranging from "very positive" to "neither" to "very nega-

The Hassan II Mosque rises over Casablanca, Morocco. Two-thirds of people polled in Morocco felt that the values of western society have a negative impact on their own society.

tive." Most of those who answered felt that the western influence was negative.

In Jordan, a country that is considered moderate and friendly by the United States, 74 percent of those who responded said that western influence was negative—53 percent "very negative," 21

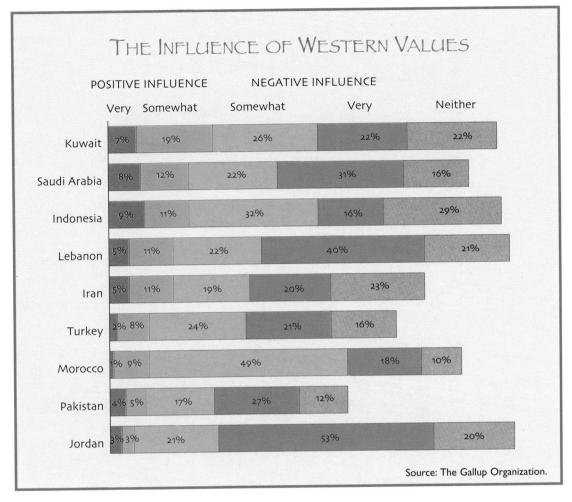

THE INFLUENCE OF WESTERN VALUES

	POSITIVE INFLUENCE		NEGATIVE INFLUENCE		
	Very	Somewhat	Somewhat	Very	Neither
Kuwait	7%	19%	26%	22%	22%
Saudi Arabia	8%	12%	22%	31%	16%
Indonesia	9%	11%	32%	16%	29%
Lebanon	5%	11%	22%	40%	21%
Iran	5%	11%	19%	20%	23%
Turkey	2%	8%	24%	21%	16%
Morocco	1%	9%	49%	18%	10%
Pakistan	4%	5%	17%	27%	12%
Jordan	3%	3%	21%	53%	20%

Source: The Gallup Organization.

The Gallup Organization asked, "How positively or negatively do you think our own value system is being influenced by the value system that prevails in the Western societies?" As this chart reflects, in every country the views of Muslims toward the United States were more negative than positive.

percent "somewhat negative." Just 6 percent felt the Western influence was positive, while 20 percent answered "neither." In Morocco, 67 percent felt that western influence is negative (18 percent "very," 49 percent "somewhat"), while this was the case among 62 percent of Lebanese respondents (40 percent "very," 22 percent "somewhat"). In Morocco, less than 1 percent of the respondents felt that western values have a "very positive" influence—the lowest figure in the survey.

The lowest percentage of people with a negative opinion of western values was in Iran, a country where more than 20 years ago the people overthrew the western-supported government of the shah and replaced it with an Islamic theocracy. In Iran, 39 percent of respondents felt a negative influence of western values (20 percent "very," 19 percent "somewhat").

The country with the highest percent of respondents that favored western values was Kuwait, at 26 percent (7 percent "very positive," 19 percent "somewhat positive"). This was still significantly lower than the 48 percent of Kuwaitis that felt western values have a negative influence. Indonesia was next, with 20 percent feeling that western values have a positive effect (9 percent "very," 12 percent "somewhat"), with Saudi Arabia also at 20 percent (8 percent "very," 12 percent "somewhat"), and Lebanon and Iran at 16 percent (in both countries, 5 percent felt the impact was "very positive," while 11 percent found it "somewhat positive").

In Turkey, perhaps the one country studied in the Gallup survey that is most similar socially to a European state, just 10 percent of the population felt that western values have a positive influence (2 percent "very," 8 percent "somewhat"). By contrast, 45 percent of Turks felt that western values have a negative influence (21 percent "very," 24 percent "somewhat").

"The image that dominates respondents' negative perceptions of the West is clear-cut: the immoral lifestyles, a weakening of family structure, a decline in social courtesy, and the loss of traditional deference to elders in Western nations," notes the Gallup Organization. "Over half of those interviewed in Jordan, Lebanon, and Kuwait mention these types of negative social influences as the aspect of the West they most resent, as do large numbers of Pakistanis and Iranians."

Two other questions asked by the Gallup Organization were, "What, if anything, do you, yourself, like best or admire most about the West," and "What, if anything, do you, yourself, like least, admire the least, or resent about the West." These questions were open-ended, meaning that the respondents had to answer in their own words, rather than selecting from a list of characteristics.

The pollsters found respondents were most likely to admire the West for its scientific and technological expertise, particularly in the area of advanced technology. This was the answer given by more than half of the people interviewed in Indonesia, Kuwait, and Iran, and by nearly half of the people interviewed in Jordan and Morocco. Other positive qualities included admiration for western political values and structures; respect for human rights; freedom and democracy; the West's level of economic advancement; cultural appreciation of the value of time; the educational level attained by individuals in the West; and the creativity, reli-

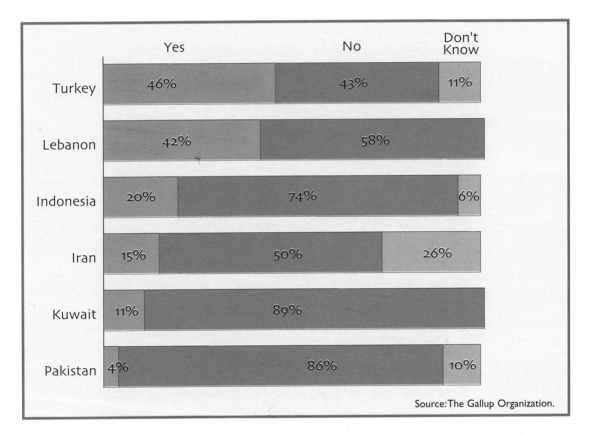

Source: The Gallup Organization.

The Gallup Organization asked, "According to news reports, groups of Arabs carried out the attacks against the USA on September 11. Do you believe this to be true or not?" In no nation included in the survey did a majority of those surveyed consider this an accurate statement. A significant majority of respondents did not say who they thought was responsible; the responses of those who did fell into four major categories: Osama bin Laden and al-Qaeda, the United States itself, Israel, and non-Muslim terrorists.

ability, and way of thinking characteristic of Western society.

Respondents were most likely to dislike the decline in Western moral values, or the high rates of alcohol and drug abuse and of crime, violence, and corruption. In addition, respondents also mentioned that they resent what they perceive as a negative Western attitude toward Muslims or Arabs. The most frequently volunteered sources of resentment of the West are perceptions that Westerners:

- are arrogant and believe their societies and civilization are more superior and advanced

- are excessively prone to interfere in the internal and political affairs of other nations

- are insufficiently attached to their own religion, religious beliefs, and ethnicity

VIEWS ON TERRORISM

People in the West often link terrorism to Muslims, particularly in the aftermath of the September 11, 2001, attacks on the World Trade Center and the Pentagon. Western perceptions of Islam have been shaped by media coverage of suicide bombings in Israel and the occupied territories, by the violence of the 1979 Iranian Revolution, and by attacks on U.S. targets like the 1993 World Trade Center bombing, the 1998 attack on U.S. embassies in Kenya and Tanzania, and the 2000 blast that damaged the U.S. warship *Cole* in the harbor at Aden, Yemen.

The truth is, however, that most Muslims do not support terrorism, and the perception that many Muslims are terrorists is unfair and incorrect. Terrorism and other forms of violence happen throughout the world, not just among Muslims. Historically, many groups and organizations throughout the world have used terrorism as a political tool. Even today there are many non-Muslim terrorist groups—the IRA and various Ulster loyalist groups in Northern Ireland; Basque separatists in Spain; rebel guerrillas like FARC and ELN in Colombia; and leftist organiza-

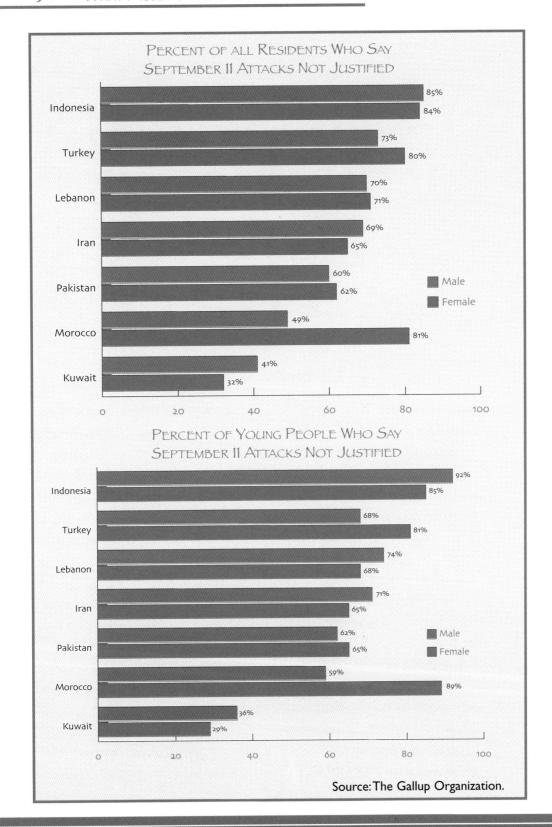

PERCENT OF ALL RESIDENTS WHO SAY
SEPTEMBER 11 ATTACKS NOT JUSTIFIED

Indonesia — Male 85% / Female 84%
Turkey — Male 73% / Female 80%
Lebanon — Male 70% / Female 71%
Iran — Male 69% / Female 65%
Pakistan — Male 60% / Female 62%
Morocco — Male 49% / Female 81%
Kuwait — Male 41% / Female 32%

PERCENT OF YOUNG PEOPLE WHO SAY
SEPTEMBER 11 ATTACKS NOT JUSTIFIED

Indonesia — Male 92% / Female 85%
Turkey — Male 68% / Female 81%
Lebanon — Male 74% / Female 68%
Iran — Male 71% / Female 65%
Pakistan — Male 62% / Female 65%
Morocco — Male 59% / Female 89%
Kuwait — Male 36% / Female 29%

Source: The Gallup Organization.

tions like Tupac Amaru in Peru. There have even been terrorist attacks carried out by Americans in the United States, such as the 1995 bombing of a federal office building in Oklahoma City.

Most Muslims agree that their religion forbids the killing of innocent civilians. They cite scripture passages like Qur'an 2: 190, which commands believers to "fight for the sake of God those that fight against you, but do not attack them first. God does not love the aggressors."

"Peace is the essence of Islam," says Prince El Hassan bin Talal of Jordan, a descendent of Muhammad. "Respecting the sanctity of life is the cornerstone of our faith." Saudi Arabia's highest authority on Islamic law, Shaikh Abdulaziz Al-Ashaikh, agrees. Shortly after the September 11 attacks, he said, "The recent developments in the United States, including hijacking planes, terrorizing innocent people, and shedding blood, constitute a form of injustice that cannot be tolerated by Islam, which views them as gross crimes and sinful acts."

Nevertheless, the issue of terrorism is a major problem confronting the Islamic world today. The debate over the causes of terrorism heated up considerably after the September 11 attacks. Some believe Muslim terrorists act out of frustration with the lack of freedom and economic opportunities in their countries. Others see terrorism as inspired by religious fervor or anger at Western colonialism and oppression.

Muslim terrorists sometimes justify their actions by claiming that they are supported by Islam. Islamic terrorists introduced Americans to the Arabic word *jihad*, which is usually translated as "holy war." But *jihad* actually means any effort to support Islam or do what is right for a Muslim, not necessarily a war. Some Islamic terrorists, including Osama bin Laden, have called on Muslims to carry out terrorist attacks; bin Laden has issued what he calls *fatwas*, or official religious declarations, condemning the West and encouraging terrorism. Only legitimate Islamic religious leaders can proclaim *fatwas*, however, and they only do so to settle a difference of opinion on religious matters. Even before the

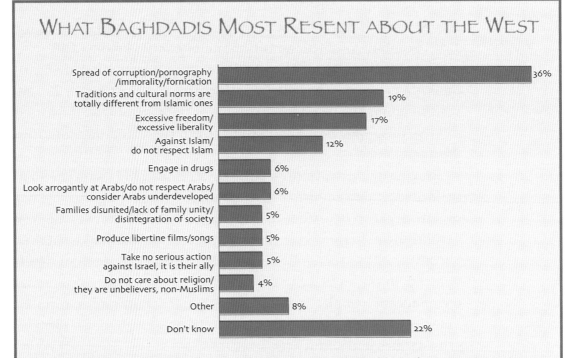

WHAT BAGHDADIS MOST RESENT ABOUT THE WEST

Spread of corruption/pornography /immorality/fornication	36%
Traditions and cultural norms are totally different from Islamic ones	19%
Excessive freedom/ excessive liberality	17%
Against Islam/ do not respect Islam	12%
Engage in drugs	6%
Look arrogantly at Arabs/do not respect Arabs/ consider Arabs underdeveloped	6%
Families disunited/lack of family unity/ disintegration of society	5%
Produce libertine films/songs	5%
Take no serious action against Israel, it is their ally	5%
Do not care about religion/ they are unbelievers, non-Muslims	4%
Other	8%
Don't know	22%

In August 2003, Gallup Organization researchers conducted hour-long, in-person interviews with a representative sample of 1,178 adults living in Iraq's capital, Baghdad. Questions covered a variety of topics currently affecting Baghdadis. In November 2003 the Gallup Organization released the results of a poll on what citizens of Baghdad resent most about the West. This was asked as an open-ended question—"In your own words, what do you most resent about the West? Anything else?"

These examples of actual responses provide further insight into Baghdadis' views about Western culture:

"Their religion is totally different from ours and they hate Islam very much."
   —woman, late 30s, basic education

"They have an educated and advanced society, but it's morally disintegrated."
   —woman, late 20s, basic education

"We heard from people who traveled there that they have great deal of
   moral corruption."
   —woman over age 60, basic education

"They disseminate corruption and do not adhere to religious values."
   —man, early 50s, intermediate education

"All their behavior is bad—not accepted by our religion. They dress indecently, and walk
   in the streets wearing obnoxious clothing."
   —man, early 30s, secondary education

"More modern than they ought to be with respect to clothing and drinking."
   —woman, early 30s, secondary education

Source: The Gallup Organization.

September 11 attacks, leaders like Abdulaziz Al-Ashaikh said that Islam forbids suicide terrorist attacks.

Yet even religious leaders who believe that Islam forbids terrorism have sometimes made exceptions out of fear of governments or others who support the terrorists' cause, and there are also Muslims in America who sympathize with terrorists. Most Muslim religious authorities and everyday Muslims alike believe that Islam does not justify terrorism. Convincing their fellow Muslims who support terrorism—and the people outside of the Islamic world who live in fear of terrorists—is a difficult but important job.

When the Gallup Organization polled the countries of the Islamic world, in six out of seven countries large majorities of the people said the September 11 attacks on the United States were not justified. In Kuwait, opinions on the attacks were divided almost evenly between those who felt the attacks were justified and those who did not. (The governments of Saudi Arabia and Jordan did not permit questions about the September 11 attacks to be asked in their countries.)

CONCLUSION

Westerners who know little about Muslims need to learn more about the Islamic world. Muslims need to learn more about Americans and the West. Both groups will soon find that they have much more in common than they thought.

The first step in understanding is to eliminate the misunderstanding and hatred that keep each group from learning the truth about the other. After the September 11 attacks, many U.S. citizens were angry and wanted revenge. Innocent Muslim Americans were targeted for violence, even though such leaders as President George W. Bush urged Americans not to attack their fellow citizens. At the same time, it is obvious that people in Muslim countries do not see world events in the same way that Americans do.

Muslim Americans come together for Friday prayers in a New York mosque. The Muslim community in the United States is growing in importance.

To learn more about each other, both groups should examine their beliefs about the other and not allow anger to disrupt their thoughts. A person who wants to better understand the Islamic world and its people better should ask himself or herself several questions:

Because the Islamic world is very large and complex, and the lives and views of Muslims differ, am I being careful not to judge all Muslims by what I learn about a few?

Am I accepting everything I hear or read as the truth without thinking, or am I considering the information with a critical eye?

Do the facts I have learned so far make a complete picture, or is something missing?

Am I learning from people or books that are dishonest, uninformed, outdated, or irrational, or am I seeking out reliable sources, such as trustworthy books and teachers, experts, and Muslims themselves?

Both the Islamic world and the West would benefit by working to understand each other better and searching for commonalities that bring cooperation, whether it is between nations or neighbors. Across the United States and around the world, students and others are beginning the search by reaching out to their neighbors and making an effort to learn more about other people and their cultures.

Chronology

610   Muhammad receives the first revelations from Allah, which will later be recorded in the Qur'an.

613   Muhammad begins publicly preaching Allah's message.

622   Muhammad and his followers begin the *hijra*, or migration, from Mecca to Medina, an event that marks the beginning of the Muslim era.

630   An Arab Muslim army led by Muhammad takes control of Mecca.

632   Muhammad dies, and the era of the "rightly guided caliphs" begins when Abu Bakr is chosen as the first caliph.

656   Ali becomes the fourth caliph, sparking a civil war in the Muslim community.

661   Ali is assassinated, and Muawiyya declares himself caliph. Ali's supporters, the Shiites, continue to support his sons' claim to the caliphate.

680   Ali's son Hussein is killed, with his family and many supporters, at the Battle of Karbala.

683   The Umayyad succession of caliphs begins. Based in Syria, their rule extends eastward to the borders of India and China and westward to Spain.

749   The Abbasids overthrow the Umayyads.

820   al-Shafii, who created an authoritative methodology for developing *Sharia*, dies.

874   The power of the Abbasid caliphs begins to wane; local dynasties start to establish rule throughout the Abbasid empire.

1058   The jurist and mystic al-Ghazali is born; he eventually helps make Sufism accepted by mainstream Islam.

Chronology

1099   The European Crusaders capture Jerusalem and establish four Crusader kingdoms.

1187   Muslim forces under Saladin defeat the Crusaders and recapture Jerusalem.

1453   The armies of the Ottoman Turks capture Constantinople, bringing the thousand-year rule of the Byzantine empire to an end.

1502   The Safavid Empire is established in Iran; Shia Islam becomes the state religion.

1526   The Moghul Empire is founded in India.

1765   Great Britain forces the Moghul emperor to give up control of part of India; the British will eventually control all of the area of modern-day India and Pakistan.

1919   In the conference that ends World War I, the Arab lands of the defeated Ottoman empire are divided into small states and placed under the control of France or Great Britain.

1923   Turkey establishes the first secular government in a Muslim country.

1928   Hasan al-Banna founds the Muslim Brotherhood in Egypt.

1941   Mawlana Abu al-Ala Mawdudi establishes the Islamic Society in India.

1947   Pakistan is created as an Islamic state.

1948   Israel is founded, and immediately fights a two-year war for independence with its neighbors.

1967   Israel defeats the combined forces of Egypt, Jordan, and Syria in the Six-Day War.

Chronology

1978   U.S. President Jimmy Carter helps to negotiate a historic peace treaty between Israel and Egypt.

1979   Revolution grips Iran and the Islamic Republic comes to power.

1980   Iraq invades Iran, setting off an eight-year conflict in the Persian Gulf.

1991   An international coalition of nations, led by the United States, attacks Iraq, forcing it to withdraw from Kuwait, which it had invaded and annexed in 1990.

1993   After secret negotiations in Oslo, Norway, representatives of Israel and the Palestinians establish a framework for an end to violence and the eventual establishment of an autonomous Palestinian state.

1995   During ethnic fighting in Bosnia, Serbian troops overrun a U.N. "safe area" at Srebrenica; an estimated 7,000 Muslim men and boys are massacred and buried in mass graves.

2000   The Israeli-Palestinian peace process fails, and the second *intifada* begins.

2001   On September 11, terrorists crash hijacked airplanes into the World Trade Center in New York and the Pentagon near Washington, D.C.; the U.S. responds by attacking Afghanistan and overthrowing the Taliban regime, which had sheltered the al-Qaeda terrorist network. This action is condemned by many Muslims.

2003   In March, the United States attacks Iraq to remove Saddam Hussein from power.

2005   The U.S. plans to hand over control of Iraq to an elected government.

Glossary

Allah—the Arabic word for "God."

caliph—Arabic for "successor." A title held by the leader of the Muslims, which is no longer used today.

Crusades—a series of invasions of the Middle East by Europeans beginning in the 11th century to seize areas holy to Christians from the hands of Muslims.

Eid al-Fitr—a holiday feast that marks the end of Ramadan.

Hadith—a collection of statements and actions by Muhammad that Muslims use to follow his example.

hajj—a journey to Mecca, where Islam began, that every Muslim is expected to make.

imam—a religious leader associated with a mosque (for Shiites, the historical leaders of Islam who followed in the footsteps of Muhammad).

Islam—from an Arabic word meaning "submitted" to God, this is the religion founded by Muhammad in the 7th century C.E.

Islamist—a Muslim activist who wants to make Islam the center of social and political life in Islamic countries.

jihad—an Arabic word meaning "striving" or doing your best in the service of Islam, including fighting in a war, but usually translated in English as simply "holy war."

mosque—a Muslim house of worship, also known in Arabic as a masjid.

Muslim—a person whose religion is Islam

Glossary

Qur'an—the holy book of Islam viewed by Muslims as a direct message from God through Muhammad.

Polygamy—marriage in which a spouse of either sex may have more than one mate at the same time.

Polygyny—the practice of having more than one wife or female mate at one time.

Ramadan—the ninth month in the Islamic calendar when Muslims refrain from eating or drinking during daylight hours.

Sharia—a traditional system of Islamic law based on the Qur'an, the opinion of Islamic leaders, and the desires of the community.

Shiite—one of the 14 percent of Muslims who follows the Shi'a branch of Islam, which began when some early Muslims followed Muhammad's son-in-law Ali as his successor instead of the leader chosen by the rest.

Sunni—a Muslim who belongs to the largest branch of Islam, which holds that Muslims should follow the *Sunna*, or way, of Muhammad, a tradition that began when the earliest Muslims chose Muhammad's successor.

Further Reading

Belt, Don, editor. *The World of Islam*. Washington, DC: National Geographic, 2001.

Esposito, John L. *What Everyone Needs to Know about Islam*. New York: Oxford University Press, 2002.

Haley, Alex, and Malcom X. *The Autobiography of Malcom X*. New York: Ballantine Books, 1990.

Hasan, Asma Gull. *American Muslims: The New Generation*. New York: Continuum, 2002.

Jordan, Michael. *Islam: An Illustrated History*. London: Carlton Books, 2002.

Miller, John, and Aaron Kenedi, editors. *Inside Islam: The Faith, the People, and the Conflicts of the World's Fastest Growing Religion*. New York: Marlowe and Co., 2002.

Nimer, Mohamed. *The North American Muslim Resource Guide: Muslim Community Life in the United States and Canada*. New York: Routledge, 2002.

Internet Resources

http://islam.about.com

A comprehensive guide to Islamic faith, culture, and life. Includes links to other resources.

http://www.infoplease.com/spot/islam.html

An easy-to-use resource for information on history, culture, and geography. Includes a quiz to test your knowledge of the Muslim world.

http://www.infoplease.com/countries.html

A convenient source of basic information about any country in the world, plus articles and tables with world and regional data.

http://www.holidays.net/ramadan

All about the celebration of the Muslim month of fasting and reflection and other information about Islam.

http://www.zawaj.com/

This matchmaking service for Muslims includes several useful resources about Muslim family life, including descriptions and pictures of traditional weddings in many Muslim countries, articles by Muslim teens about issues they care about, and recipes for food enjoyed by Muslims across the world.

http://www.cair-net.org

The website of the Council on American Islamic Relations, which works to represent Muslim views on important issues and foster better relations between Muslims and mainstream America.

Index

Abraham, 15, 33–34, 72
Abu Bakr, 22
Adam, 33
Afghanistan, 13, 40, 45, 66–67, 71, 85
al-Hajar al-Aswad, 33–34
Al-Haram al-Sharif, *71*
Algeria, 25, 39, 41, 66
Ali, *21*, 22, 38
bin Ali, Sharif Hussein, 75
Allah, 15–16, 19, 20, 30, 33
   See also Islam
Arab League, 78
Arafat, Yasir, 80, 81–82
arranged marriage, 44, *47*, 48
   See also marriage
art, Islamic, 31
Al-Ashaikh, Shaikh Abdulaziz, 95, 97
Azerbaijan, 22

Baghdad, Iraq, *96*
Bahrain, 22, 40, 69
Balfour, Arthur James Lord, 75
Balfour Declaration, 75
   See also Israeli-Palestinian conflict
Bangladesh, 39, 61, 69
Barak, Ehud, 81
Battle of Karbala, *21*, *22*, 38
Begin, Menachem, *79*
Bhutto, Benazir, 61
   See also women
Brunei, 39
Burkholder, Richard W., *12*, 46
Bush, George W., 24, 82, 97

calendar, Islamic, 36–37, 38
Camp David Accords, 78–79
   See also Israeli-Palestinian conflict
Carter, Jimmy, 78, *79*

charity, 32, 36
   See also five pillars of Islam
Christianity, 15, 20, 22–24, 38, 48, 73
   See also Islam; Judaism
Clemenceau, Georges, *74*
Clinton, Bill, 80–82
Cold War, 78
   See also Soviet Union
crime, *12*
Crusades, 22–24
culture, Islamic, 20–21, 43–51, 55–59, 62
   See also Islam

divorce (*talaq*), 55–59
   See also marriage

education, 51, *52*, 53–55, *56*, 92
Egypt, 24, 39, 55, 62, 64, 69, 77, 78
Eid al-Adha, 38
   See also holidays
Eid al-Fitr, 37–38
   See also holidays
European colonization, 24–25

family life, 48–51
   See also culture, Islamic; marriage
fasting, 32–33, 37
   See also five pillars of Islam
female genital mutilation (FGM), 67–68
   See also women
five pillars of Islam, 30–34
   See also Islam
France, 24–25, *74*, 75
Freedom House, 39
fundamentalists, Islamic. See Islamists (Islamic fundamentalists)

Gallup Poll of the Islamic World, 10–13, *96*

Numbers in **bold italic** refer to captions.

Index

divorce, 57–58
education, *52*, 53–55, *56*
Israeli-Palestinian conflict, 83–85
marriage and family life, 43, 46, *47*, *50*, 51
Muslims' view of the West, *12*, 83–85, 87–93, *94*
government, 39–41
Great Britain, 24–25, *74*, 75–76
Great Mosque (Mecca), *32*, 33
Gulf War (1991), 80

Hadith, 34–35, 57
    See also Qur'an; Sunna
Hamas, 80
    See also Israeli-Palestinian conflict
Hassan, Riffat, 68
Hassan II Mosque, *89*
henna, 45
    See also marriage
holidays, 32–33, 36–38
    See also Islam
human rights, 40, 68, 80, 92
Hussein, *21*, 22, 38
Hussein, Saddam, 72

India, 22, 25, 39, 66
Indonesia, 10, 25, 26, 39, 53, *56*, 61, 64, 69, 71, 83, 84, 91, 92
intifada, 80, 81
    See also Israeli-Palestinian conflict
Iran, 10–11, 22, 26, 39, 41, 51, 61–62, 66, 71, 83, 84, 91, 92
Iraq, 13, 22, 39, 65, 71–72, *74*, 75, 85, *86*, *96*
Ishmael, 33
Islam, 98–99
    calendar, 36–37, 38
    and the Crusades, 22–24
    and culture, 20–21
    division of, into sects, 21–22
    and divorce (talaq), 55–59
    five pillars of, 30–34

founding of, 15–19
holidays of, 32–33, 36–38
and the Israeli-Palestinian conflict, 82–85
law (Sharia), 38–39, 41, 57, 66, 67, 95
and marriage and family life, 43–51, 62
population of followers, 9–10
spread of, 19–20
and the United States, 24–27, 40, 41, 53, 71–72, 78–85, 87–93, 96, 97–99
and Western values, 88–93, *96*
and women, *35*, 36, 40, 41, 46, *47*, 53–57, 58–59, 61–69
    See also Christianity; Gallup Poll of the Islamic World; Judaism
Islamists (Islamic fundamentalists), 40–41
    See also government
Israel, 71, 72–73, 76–80, 82, *92*
Israeli-Palestinian conflict, 78–82
    Muslim views on the, 82–85
    roots of the, 71–77
    See also Israel; Palestine
Italy, 24, *74*

Jerusalem, 23, 24, *71*, 72, 76, 77, 81, 82
    See also Israeli-Palestinian conflict
Jordan, 10, 25, 39, 46, 48, 51, 53, 57–58, 65, 77–78, 80, 83, 84, 89–90, 92, 95, 97
Judaism, 15, 20, 38, 72–76
    See also Christianity; Islam
June 1967 War, 77, 78
    See also Israeli-Palestinian conflict

Kaaba, *32*, 33–34
Khadimiya Shrine, *9*
Khomeini, Ayatollah Ruhollah, 41
Kuwait, 10, 39, 46, 48, 51, 53, 55, 57, 59, 83, 91, 92, 97

bin Laden, Osama, 85, *92*, 95
    See also terrorism
Lebanon, 10, 22, 25, 46, 48, 51, 53, 57–59, 65, 66,

Index

74, 75, 77–78, 83–84, 90, 91
Lloyd George, David, **74**

Malaysia, 45, 64
marriage, 43–48, 62
    See also culture, Islamic; divorce (talaq);
        family life
Mecca, 16–17, 19, 33–34, 37, 38
Medina, 17, 19, 37
Morocco, 10, 39, 51, 53, 55, 66, 69, 83, 84, **89**, 90,
    92
Mossadegh, Mohammed, 26
Muhammad, 15–17, 19, 22, 30, **31**, 32–35, 37, 57,
    62
    See also Islam
Muslims
    attitudes of, toward the West, **12**, 83–85,
        87–93, **94**
    population, 9–10
    See also Islam

Netanyahu, Benjamin, 80–81
Newport, Frank, 87–88
Nigeria, 57, 67

Oman, 40, 69
Organization of the Islamic Conference, 67
Orlando, Signor, **74**
Oslo Accords, 81–82
    See also Israeli-Palestinian conflict
Ottoman Empire, 25, 75

Pakistan, 10, 22, 39, 51, 53, 55, 57, 61, 83, 84
Palestine, 45, 72, 73–77, 79–80, 82, 83
    See also Israeli-Palestinian conflict
Palestine Liberation Organization (PLO), 77–78,
    80
    See also Israeli-Palestinian conflict
Palestinian Authority, 80–81
    See also Israeli-Palestinian conflict
Pan Arab Research Center, 10

pilgrimage (hajj), 33–34, 38
    See also five pillars of Islam
polygamy, 45–46, **47**, 48
    See also marriage
population, Muslim, 9–10
prayer, 30–31, **37**, 48–49, **98**
    See also five pillars of Islam

al-Qaeda, 40, 85, 92
    See also terrorism
Qatar, 40, 69
Qur'an, 15, **18**, 19, 20, 29, 34–36, 53, **56**, 62–64, **68**
    and polygamy, 45–46
    and Sharia (Islamic law), 38
        See also Hadith; Islam; Sunna

Rabin, Yitzhak, 80
Ramadan, 32–33, 37
    See also holidays
Richard the Lionhearted, 24
    See also Crusades
Roman Empire, 72–73
    See also Israeli-Palestinian conflict

Saad, Lydia, 83, 85
Sadat, Anwar, 78, **79**
Saudi Arabia, 10–11, 34, 36, 39, 40, 46, 51, 53, 55,
    57, 59, **61**, 64, 66, 83, 91, 95, 97
September 11, 2001, **92**, 93, **94**, 95, 97
    See also terrorism
Sharia (Islamic law), 38–39, 41, 57, 66, 67, 95
Shia Islam, **21**, **22**, 35, 38, 41
    See also Islam
Soviet Union, 25, 78, 88
Spain, 22
Sudan, 39, 45, 67
Sukarno, Achmad, 26
Sunna, 34–36
    See also Hadith; Qur'an
Sunni Islam, 22, 35
    See also Islam

Index

Sykes-Picot agreement, 25, 75
　　See also Israeli-Palestinian conflict
Syria, 22, 39, 65, *74*, 75, 77

bin Talal, El Hassan, 95
Taliban, 13, 40, 66–67, 85
　　See also Afghanistan
terrorism, *11*, 24, 40, *92*, 93–95, 97
Transjordan, 75
　　See also Jordan
Tunisia, 39, 45, 66
Turkey, 10, 25, 39, 41, 51, 55, 61, 64, 66, 69, 83, 91

umma (community), 17–19
United Arab Emirates, 45
United Nations, 76
United States, 53
　　and the Israeli-Palestinian conflict, 71–72,
　　　78–85
　　views of, in the Muslim world, 24–27, 40,
　　　41, 83–85, 87–93, *96*, 97–99
Urban II (Pope), 23
Uzbekistan, *43*

values. See Western values
veiling, *35*, 36, 64–67
　　See also women

Wahhabism, 39
　　See also Islam
Western values, 88–93
　　See also United States
Wilson, Woodrow, *74*
Wolfe, Michael, 34
women, 40, 41, 61–69
　　and divorce, 56–57, 58–59
　　and education, 53–55
　　and polygamy, 46, *47*
　　and veiling, *35*, 36, 64–67
World War I, 25, *74*, 75
World War II, 25, 76, 88

Yathrib. See Medina
Yemen, 36, 45

Zionism, 74–75, 76
　　See also Israeli-Palestinian conflict

Picture Credits

Contributors

General Editor DR. KHALED ABOU EL FADL is one of the leading authorities in Islamic law in the United States and Europe. He is currently a visiting professor at Yale Law School as well as Professor of Law at the University of California, Los Angeles (UCLA). He serves on the Board of Directors of Human Rights Watch, and regularly works with various human rights organizations, such as the Lawyer's Committee for Human Rights and Amnesty International. He often serves as an expert witness in international litigation involving Middle Eastern law, and in cases involving terrorism, national security, immigration law and political asylum claims.

Dr. Abou El Fadl's books include *The Place of Tolerance in Islam* (2002); *Conference of the Books: The Search for Beauty in Islam* (2001); *Rebellion in Islamic Law* (2001); *Speaking in God's Name: Islamic Law, Authority, and Women* (2001); and *And God Knows the Soldiers: The Authoritative and Authoritarian in Islamic Discourse* (second edition, revised and expanded, 2001).

Dr. Abou El Fadl was trained in Islamic legal sciences in Egypt, Kuwait, and the United States. After receiving his bachelors degree from Yale University and law degree from the University of Pennsylvania, he clerked for Arizona Supreme Court Justice J. Moeller. While in graduate school at Princeton University, where he earned a Ph.D. in Islamic Law he practiced immigration and investment law in the United States and the Middle East. Before joining the UCLA faculty in 1998, he taught at the University of Texas at Austin, Yale Law School, and Princeton University.

General Editor DR. SHAMS INATI is Professor of Islamic Studies at Villanova University. She is a specialist in Islamic philosophy and theology and has published widely in the field. Her publications include *Remarks and Admonitions, Part One: Logic* (1984), *Our Philosophy* (1987), *Ibn Sina and Mysticism* (1996), *The Second Republic of Lebanon* (1999), *The Problem of Evil: Ibn Sina's Theodicy* (2000), and *Iraq: Its History, People, and Politics* (2003). She has also written a large number of articles that have appeared in books, journals, and encyclopedias.

Dr. Inati has been the recipient of a number of awards and honors, including an Andrew Mellon Fellowship, an Endowment for the Humanities grant, a U.S. Department of Defense grant, and a Fulbright grant. For further information about her work, see www.homepage.villanova.edu/shams.inati.

RICK HODGES studied government and foreign affairs at the University of Virginia. He earned a master's degree in political science at George Washington University in Washington, D.C., where he has worked as an author, journalist, lobbyist, and fundraiser. His travels have taken him to Islamic sites in Kenya and Zanzibar, the homes of Muslim families in the United States, and his own community's mosque. He lives with his wife and daughter in Arlington, Virginia.